Captivating Campuses

Proven Practices that Promote College Student Persistence, Engagement, and Success

Nicholas D. Young
Christine N. Michael
Jennifer A. Smolinski

Series in Education
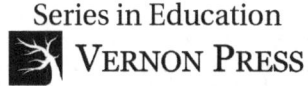
VERNON PRESS

Copyright © 2019 Vernon Press, an imprint of Vernon Art and Science Inc, on behalf of the author.

All rights reserved. No part of this publication may be reproduced, stored in a retrieval system, or transmitted in any form or by any means, electronic, mechanical, photocopying, recording, or otherwise, without the prior permission of Vernon Art and Science Inc.

www.vernonpress.com

In the Americas:
Vernon Press
1000 N West Street,
Suite 1200, Wilmington,
Delaware 19801
United States

In the rest of the world:
Vernon Press
C/Sancti Espiritu 17,
Malaga, 29006
Spain

Series in Education

Library of Congress Control Number: 2019930750

ISBN: 978-1-62273-714-7

Also available:

Hardback: 978-1-62273-613-3

E-book: 978-1-62273-643-0

Product and company names mentioned in this work are the trademarks of their respective owners. While every care has been taken in preparing this work, neither the authors nor Vernon Art and Science Inc. may be held responsible for any loss or damage caused or alleged to be caused directly or indirectly by the information contained in it.

Every effort has been made to trace all copyright holders, but if any have been inadvertently overlooked the publisher will be pleased to include any necessary credits in any subsequent reprint or edition.

Cover design by Vernon Press.

Table of Contents

Acknowledgement   v

Preface   vii

Chapter One
**Connecting to Campus: Theories and
Requisites for College Student Engagement**   1

Chapter Two
**Student and Campus Challenges:
Contemporary Solutions to Engagement**   21

Chapter Three
**Preparation for Postsecondary Success:
Promoting Positive Campus Transitions**   35

Chapter Four
**Leadership for Learning:
Leveraging Potential in all Students**   45

Chapter Five
**Connections Outside of the Classroom:
Building College-Community Partnerships**   55

Chapter Six
**Advancing Academic Advising: Assets-Based
Approaches to Student Development**   65

Chapter Seven
**Inviting and Potent Instruction:
Best Practices to Cultivate Learning**   95

Chapter Eight
**Beyond Academics: Enhancing the Educational
Experience through Extracurricular Activities**   107

Chapter Nine
**Educational Equity: Promoting
Access and Success for Diverse Students** 117

Chapter Ten
**Passion and Purpose: Engaged
Students Need Engaged Faculty and Advisors** 129

References 153

About the Authors 171

Acknowledgement

Writing a book is a challenging undertaking—it takes considerable time, research and the support of important people in your life to convert thoughts to words according to the rules of the English language while remaining consistent with the American Psychological Association's writing style guidelines. We were blessed to have had a strong cheerleader and talented editor in Mrs. Suzanne "Sue" Clark who supported this project from beginning to end. Whether offering gentle reminders that she was waiting on the manuscript (which was a nudge to finally finish) or completing the arduous task of copyediting the draft version, she was an essential member of our writing team. There is no question that Sue's careful review and valuable suggestions enhanced this book considerably and made it publication-ready. We are, then, grateful for her substantial contributions and wish all to know that she is a talented and capable writer and professional in her own right. The fact that she is also one of the nicest, kindest people we know made collaborating with her an added bonus.

Preface

Captivating Campuses: Proven Practices that Promote College Student Persistence, Engagement, and Success is written for higher education administrators and faculty, student services personnel, and graduate students studying higher education leadership. Mainly, however, this is a book for those who are committed to seeing all college students succeed through being actively engaged in their own education. While this book largely focuses on understanding the role that student engagement plays in educational achievement on the post-secondary campus, it approaches that broad topic with a clear understanding that there are countless factors that affect each student's ability and motivation to engage with the full college experience, both in and outside of the classroom.

The word "captivating" means capable of attracting and holding one's interest (Merriam-Webster, 2018). That is precisely the state of being necessary for contemporary college students to navigate the often turbulent waters of obtaining their degree. Students need to be captivated by at least some element of their college experience—classroom, dorm, athletic, leadership, extracurricular, service activities, to name a few—in order to form a bond with their institution and feel motivated and attached enough to put in the hard work over two, four or more years until graduation.

A great deal has been written about the relationship between student engagement with and feelings of connectedness to their college campus and persistence to graduation. Historically, and still today, there are particular groups of students who regularly take advantage of engagement activities; however, on the margins of any learning community, are tens of thousands of students who cannot or choose not to fully engage.

Post-secondary institutions must make a concerted effort to listen to the needs and experiences of such students in order to program effectively for maximal involvement. For those who are part-time, commuters, non-traditional or members of marginalized groups, full engagement can be hampered by myriad variables to include social discomfort, transportation, finances, the need for childcare, poor academic preparation, disabilities, or other conditions that the students themselves experience as alienating.

Campuses that captivate their students' interests and passions and provide spaces for them to exhibit leadership, socialize with diverse others, form meaningful relationships with their faculty, and matter to peers and personnel have a far greater chance of both retaining their students to graduation and helping them develop as whole human beings who will contribute fully to their communities and society at large.

The motivation for writing this book comes from several concerns:

- *Our recognition that student engagement is the key to positive outcomes during the college years;*
- *Our concern that while access to post-secondary education has increased, graduation rates, especially for historically underserved groups, have not;*
- *Our awareness that student engagement is multifaceted, involving cognitive, social, emotional, and psychological domains;*
- *Our belief that both higher education institutions and college students share equal responsibility for offering and participating in academic and social experiences that enrich classroom learning;*
- *Our knowledge that there is leadership potential inherent in all students and that a campus that builds and nurtures inclusive student leadership helps students thrive;*
- *Our understanding that all meaningful learning is interdependent and relational and that there are particular strategies that increase engagement of learners, including opportunities for collaborative work, reflection, writing, problem-solving and global applications of knowledge;*
- *Our awareness that involvement in even one extracurricular activity, club, team, or community project increases student engagement and commitment to the institution;*
- *Our study of the most effective engagement practices over years of experience in higher education and the recognition that there are proven approaches to building connections that keep students on campus.*

The book includes chapters on the many facets of student engagement. It attempts to define student engagement, differentiating it from involvement, and covers seminal theories of college student engagement. As the second chapter indicates, the actual preparation for and transition to college is critical for positive academic and social success—both of which are linked to engagement with the life of the campus. Chapters also discuss the powerful role that relationships play in helping students identify their interests and talents and find venues for their exploration and expression during the college experience. The connections formed with peers, college personnel, advisors/mentors, and faculty all influence a student's sense that s/he matters on campus, is valued as a unique individual, and would be missed if s/he departed.

Other chapters include discussions and examples of best practice when it comes to creating engaging classroom experiences. National research on college student engagement, conducted over many years, consistently highlights effective practices. Among these are service learning, collaborative projects with peers, research with faculty, study abroad, study as part of a living/learning community, inquiry-based learning, the use of technology, and learning that is situated in real-life problems that are of importance to the student.

Faculty and advisors, as well as coaches, residence life and other student services personnel, as well as mentors may be the key to whether students are retained or lost. This book reviews some of the latest thinking on academic advising and its expanded role in college student development. Given that faculty and advisors face an ever-expanding population of learners, issues of educational equity, culturally-competent practice, and diversity in learning and cultural styles also populate the chapters. While once these learners might have been termed "marginalized," "at-risk," or historically "underserved," theorists and researchers presented in this tome advocate for college personnel to consider that all students arrive "at promise" and that it is the institution's responsibility to use proven, assets-based approaches to promoting success.

Building students' sense of academic efficacy and the personal belief that they have the skills to work through developmental issues and personal challenges on the college campus are a part of the job description of everyone on a captivating campus. Creating a strong cadre of students who can persist to successful college graduation requires the commitment of all offices, all personnel and, of course, the students themselves. Many students matriculate with a sense of academic frailty or impostership while others face social doubts as to whether they will fit in, find others with similar affinities, or blend into the culture of the college. Campuses that captivate students assure these diverse learners that they belong.

The topics noted previously are the focal points of the chapters of this book. The authors strive to balance theory, research, and data-driven best practices in the discussion of how we can make the growing numbers of students able to access higher education successful graduates of their colleges and universities. While it is exciting that expanded populations of students who once were on the fringes of college recruitment now are matriculating at our campuses, there is an ethical responsibility to provide the framework for their success. Created thoughtfully, this framework reflects individualized student engagement plans that meet the need of each unique campus.

Captivating Campuses: Proven Practices that Promote College Student Persistence, Engagement, and Success was written by an experienced team of higher education professionals. This text aims to add to the growing body of literature on college student engagement by recognizing the growing diversity on our campuses and the challenges and opportunities diverse students bring to the classroom and campus. It is our hope that those who currently practice within the realm of higher education, and those who are hoping to join the ranks, will feel an increased sense of mission to explore new aspects of creating student engagement on campus after reading this book.

Chapter One

Connecting to Campus: Theories and Requisites for College Student Engagement

All institutions of higher education aim to provide a meaningful postsecondary education, career preparation, and positive student development experiences (Quaye & Harper, 2015). They also strive to retain their students and graduate them in a timely fashion. Key to all of the aforementioned is an engaged learner, but what, exactly, promotes student engagement from the time a student matriculates to his or her successful college graduation?

Interestingly, although much research and literature centers on precollege preparation and the transition to college that students undergo, experts like Strayhorn (2012) argue that what happens in college matters more in developing engaged learners who persist to graduation. This holds true for all races and both genders (Strayhorn, 2012). Being actively engaged in activities is associated with positive learning outcomes in the arts, civic responsibility, values clarification, critical thinking, self-esteem, leadership, multicultural competence, and racial identity affiliation and expression (National Survey of Student Engagement, 2018).

There are many theories of student engagement and a variety of theorists and researchers have studied the phenomenon to determine if there are common traits of engaged learning environments, as well as engaging campus communities (Quaye & Harper, 2015). These theories are derived from many different fields—psychology, social psychology, neurobiology, human development, and education.

Defining Engagement

In general terms, the theory of engagement is based on the concept that if students find a learning activity meaningful and have a high degree of interest in tasks that comprise it, they learn more efficiently, are more apt to have retention of the learned material and can transfer what they have learned to other situations (Quaye & Harper, 2015). Teachers who want to increase the chances that their students will have this level of engagement can do so when "they provide those qualities that are most likely to appeal to the values, interests and needs of the students involved" (Schlechty Center for Leadership in School Reform, n.d., p. 6).

Ferlazzo (2011) writes about the role of involvement and engagement in interactions with parents and students in our schools, noting that there are differences between involvement and engagement. In reviewing dictionary definitions of the two terms, "*involve* is 'to enfold or envelope,' but to *engage* is 'to come together and interlock.' Involvement implies doing to; in contrast, engagement implies doing with" (Ferlazzo, 2011, p.10). Engagement involves forming a partnership with others. Although Ferlazzo (2011) was writing about PK-12 settings, this equally holds true in higher education.

In thinking of college student engagement specifically, Harper and Quaye (2015) make a clear distinction between involvement and engagement as it relates to student success in that it is absolutely possible for a student to be involved without being engaged. The important other aspect is that the student not only expends time and effort, but that s/he does so in educationally purposeful activities; thus, this definition places equal responsibility for engaged learning on both the student and the institution of higher education (Quaye & Harper, 2015).

Pascarella & Terenzini (2005) write that "the impact of college is largely determined by individual effort and involvement in the academic, interpersonal, and extracurricular offerings on campus," (p. 602) again highlighting that the student must invest personal energies, while the institution needs to offer a rich array of purposeful activities with which s/he can engage.

In order for a student to become engaged, rather than just involved, s/he must look for rich learning and developmental opportunities and invest more of him or herself in those activities; however, it also is the institution's responsibility to offer those opportunities and through skillful advising and mentorship, assist its students in setting and attaining meaningful and measurable goals (Trevino, 2018).

Astin's (1999) work expressed the notion that students who are more involved in the life of their college are more apt to feel an attachment to that institution. This definition references the amount of psychological and physical energy one expends on academic pursuits (Astin, 1999). This is, as Strayhorn (2012) points out, a definition that rests on what students do, rather than what they feel or think. Student behavior, then, indicates the level of involvement.

It is completely possible that a student may show the signs of being involved without being engaged. Quaye and Harper (2015) give the example of a student who shows up on time to every meeting of a campus organization but sits passively during those meetings, doesn't share opinions, doesn't volunteer for committees and does not step up into any leadership possibilities nor interact with other club members. One can imagine a similar scenario in a classroom.

Engagement relates specifically to both the time students spend on those educationally purposeful activities but also the energy that the institution expends to get its students to participate in activities that have been proven to lead to student success (Quaye & Harper, 2015). While it may be seen as splitting hairs, there are important distinctions between involvement and engagement. It is entirely plausible that a student could be involved in activities without being successful or be involved in activities that do not necessarily lead to student success.

Engagement also relates to how an institution of higher education allocates resources and creates opportunities and structures to encourage students to take part in activities that have been proven to lead to student success (Quaye & Harper, 2015; Robsham, 2016). These are evidence-based strategies and can take place in either the social or academic sphere.

Qualities of Engaged Students

Schlechty (2011) discovered that there are four essential traits of students who are engaged in their academic work. Such students feel an attraction to their work, they are willing to persist even if the work is challenging to them, they express pleasure or delight when they master the learning task, and they place their emphasis on optimal performance (Schlechty, 2011). Faculty members, then, should design learning activities that take these assumptions into consideration. Variations lead to differences in the degree of effort that students will expend, and students' decisions about the consequences of being engaged in the task at hand result in different types of involvement (Schlechty, 2011).

Schlechty (2011) describes different levels of student engagement, ranging from authentic to rebellious. Authentic engagement occurs when the work at hand has true meaning for and immediate value to the student (Schlechty, 2011). This should be the aim in all college classrooms. A level removed, 'ritual engagement' takes place when the learning task does not have authentic learning qualities; rather, the student sees a connection between mastering the task and earning extrinsic rewards that s/he values (Schlechty, 2011).

If students take on a learning task with passive or strategic compliance, they devote time on task only for the purpose of avoiding negative consequences; the task itself has no meaning or value for the student (Schlechty, 2011). Retreatism is the fourth level of student engagement and it is defined by a student's disengagement from the task, although s/he does not interfere with the learning environment or classroom activities. Rebellion represents a full-blown refusal to attempt the work. This final level is completely devoid of student engagement and entails the disruption of others or the learner attempts to negotiate alternative learning activities (Schlechty, 2011).

Faculty members can improve the likelihood that students will be engaged in learning activities by considering what Schlechty (2002) terms 'design qualities.' Design qualities fall into two categories, those of context and choice (Schlechty, 2002). Qualities of context are the content and substance of the course work, including the organization of knowledge; clearly articulated product standards; and protecting students from negative consequences if they fail initially (Schlechty, 2002).

Savvy faculty begin by considering the content and the level of student interest in the topic. Next, they choose the most appropriate way in which to organize the work (didactic, discovery, or problem-solving approaches, for example); and finally, they attend to individual learning styles as they may play out in the learning activities and assessment. Choices about how and when to collaborate with others, what mode of learning to engage in, and what artifacts best represent their deep understanding of content should be student determined as often as possible (Schlechty, 2002).

Why Engagement Matters

Nygaard, Brand, Bartholomew, & Millard (2013) stated simply that student engagement drives individual and institutional development. Student voice and role come together as important elements in creating an engaged culture in which learners view themselves as partners in the educational experience and where they are also able to include extracurricular activities offered by the university as means to self-development (Nygaard et al., 2013).

Finn & Zimmer (2013) believed that a heightened emphasis on student engagement arose due to a greater concern about retaining students at risk and this thinking gave way to status risk and educational risk. Status risk (conditions) are sociodemographic factors tied to lower student achievement and retention to graduation, encompassing socioeconomic status, parental educational levels, and minority status (Finn & Zimmer, 2013). Educational risks (events) describe educational outcomes that can hinder academic achievement and attainment (Finn & Zimmer, 2013).

Historically, the question of how students deemed to be at risk have succeeded has been understudied; yet, when this question has been explored, the answer seems to lie in a high degree of student engagement as "the attention…investment, and effort students expend in the work of school" (Finn & Zimmer, 2013, p. 98). Academic and social engagement are viewed as protective factors with respect to educational risk.

Quaye & Harper (2015), among others, take issue with the term 'at-risk students,' saying that it is "perhaps one of the most unfair terms used in American education" (p. 11). Using their theory, students are only at risk for disengaging or dropping out of college when

> *educators are negligent in customizing engagement efforts that connect them to the campus. While some may enter with characteristics and backgrounds that suggest they need customized services and resources, we maintain that student affairs educators and faculty should be proactive in assessing those needs and creating the environmental conditions that would enable such students to thrive* (p.11).

It is worth our time to be concerned with student engagement/disengagement for four major reasons, Finn & Zimmer (2013) argue.

- There is a clear relationship between engagement behaviors and student learning, as demonstrated by empirical research.
- Students who remain engaged academically persist to graduation, both at the K-12 and post-secondary level.
- Engagement behaviors are predictive—that is, early withdrawal in the elementary or middle school grades predicts risk of academic failure and dropping out. Students can be identified early so that interventions can begin.
- Engagement behaviors can be influenced by school and teachers; there are practices that boost engagement and lead to academic achievement and persistence.
(Finn & Zimmer, 2013)

Student engagement is positively related to GPA and persistence, as well as retention from the critical first year of college to the second and sophomore success (Webber, Krylow, & Zhang, 2013; Zobel, 2016). While smaller colleges generally are more effective at engaging students, due to a smaller student-faculty ratio, many larger institutions have employed highly effective practices. Student engagement within an institution varies more than across institutions, and student engagement in effective practices is not related to the institution's selectivity (Kuh, 2018).

Historically, certain groups of students have been found to have typically higher levels of engagement in college than others. Variables included being female, attending college full time, being part of a living/learning community, living on campus, having internship experiences, having been involved in diversity experiences and starting and finishing at the same college or university (Kuh, Kinzie, Buckley, Bridges, & Hayek, 2006). Single-mission colleges confer engagement advantages; those who graduated from all-women's colleges said that they felt challenged in the classroom, had more opportunities to engage with faculty, experienced more opportunities to be involved in classroom settings that utilized learning with others or participatory learning, and higher degrees of diversity-related experiences (Kuh et al., 2006).

Faculty made a critical difference for Hispanic students in that those institutions with greater than 10% Hispanic faculty had highly engaged Hispanic students; while Asian American and African American students reported the lowest levels of satisfaction with their institutions (Kuh et al., 2006). The best predictor of how satisfied a student was with his or her college or university was the degree to which s/he felt that the institution supported his or her needs in both the academic and social domains (Kuh et al., 2006).

Kuh et al. (2006) further argue that far too many students come to college already predisposed to disengagement because of what they term a 'cumulative deficit' in critical study skills, academic background and attitudes towards learning. An 'entitlement mentality' exists in which students feel that they need to make only a small personal investment in the learning process in order to achieve satisfactory grades. The authors cite the NESE survey that shows on average, students at the high school level devoted only six hours per week on their classes, received inflated grades, and experienced low academic expectations of them; all of these experiences led to their severe underestimation of what they would need to put forward in effort in order to be successful college graduates (Kuh et al., 2006).

The many students who matriculate with this mentality rather quickly encounter cognitive dissonance as they compare their college experience with what they think should happen; some will decide that certain activities are inappropriate, not meaningful, irrelevant, or not worth their investment of time and effort. Kuh et al. (2006) note that expectations shape a student's behaviors and experiences on campus, saying that if students matriculate without the expectation of taking part in cultural events, making social connections, or interacting with professors, they are unlikely to pursue these activities or may miss opportunities to engage. For all of the above reasons, it is imperative that college personnel consider student engagement as the key to unlocking passion, potential, and personal connection while on campus.

Prominent Theories of College Student Engagement

Csikszentmihalyi: Flow Theory

It is interesting to consider student engagement from the perspective of flow theory as students who are able to attain states of flow have demonstrated higher rates of graduation and academic achievement (Csikszentmihalyi, 1990). High levels of student engagement (concentration, attention, interest and enjoyment) were relevant predictors of continuing motivation and commitment of high school students, as well as their overall college performance. Myriad phenomenological, instructional, individual and school factors affected flow.

According to Csikszentmihalyi (1990), 'flow' occurs when an individual is deeply absorbed in an activity that is intrinsically enjoyable. In order to achieve a state of flow, students must believe that the learning activity is worth their engagement even without goal attainment (Csikszentmihalyi, 1990). They are able to function in the highest state of their capacities because the activity that they are engaged in holds intrinsic reward. Artists, athletes, and others experience flow when they take part in producing what they consider to be their optimal work or performance. Flow occurs when individuals are challenged but have the requisite skills to meet the challenge (Csikszentmihalyi, 1990). With appropriate supports, these learners could stretch beyond their abilities to experience flow; however, if there was no challenge, too much challenge, or high anxiety, flow could not be achieved (Csikszentmihalyi, 1990).

Flow rarely occurs in a passive situation, regardless of whether it is inside or outside the classroom. The autotelic individual (self-goal-setting) is formed from environments possessing five specific attributes (Csikszentmihalyi, 1990). This is similar in some ways to Maslow's (2013) self-actualizing personality. The environment must support clear expectations, practice centering, encourage choice, demonstrate commitment to the individual, and offer appropriate levels of challenge (Csikszentmihalyi, 1990; Maslow, 2013). While Csikszentmihalyi (1990) was writing about family environments, it is clear that the author's ideas can be directly translated to the college campus as well.

Kytle (2004) expressed somewhat of a concern over the concept of flow as applied to teaching, believing that it rested on a flawed dichotomy of either a state of flow or no flow. The intermediate stages between optimal experience, which is rare, and middle-range experiences, which are generally daily, are what most educators deal with (Kytle, 2004). The true educational dilemma is how to move students to the self-management of personal motivation and attention.

Tinto: Engagement and Persistence

Tinto (1993, 2000, 2012) is most frequently cited in relation to college student retention and engagement and centers on the notion that student engagement (academic and social integration, in his earliest terms) is positively correlated with persistence. Engagement, Tinto (1993) postulated, is the single most important predictor of student persistence in college. If students feel disconnected from their faculty, peers, and the administration of the institution, as well as its organizations and academic and social activities, they are at far greater risk for dropping out.

As Tinto wrote in 2000, "leavers of this type express a sense of not having made any significant contacts or not feeling membership in the institution" (p. 7). Tinto's (2000) major argument is that when students experience high levels of social and academic integration, they become committed to their institutions; thus, they are more likely to persist even during challenging times. The connections these students make offer them more resources to draw upon if and when times are difficult.

Bean and Eaton (2001) and Bean (2005) cited marginal institutional commitment as the primary factor in exiting college. When students are actively engaged in purposeful endeavors that connect them to meaningful learning and to others on campus, they feel a sense of obligation and responsibility to the institution and to persisting in their studies (Bean, 2005). When others depend on them for their roles as tutors, mentors, leaders, or team members, they experience a sense of mattering to others on campus and do not wish to let others down.

Astin: Student Involvement

Astin's (1984) theory of student involvement explains how desirable outcomes for institutions of higher education are viewed in relation to how students change and develop as a result of being involved co-curricularly. The theory is made up of three key elements to include inputs, environment, and outputs. The first springs from a student's inputs such as his or her demographics, background, previous life, and educational experiences. The second part involves the student's environment, which accounts for all of the experiences a student would have during college. Lastly, there are outcomes that cover a student's characteristics, knowledge, attitudes, beliefs, and values that exist after a student has graduated from college.

Astin (1984) also created five basic assumptions about involvement.

- Involvement requires an investment of psychosocial and physical energy.
- Involvement is continuous, and that the amount of energy invested varies from student to student.
- Aspects of involvement may be qualitative and quantitative.
- What a student gains from being involved (or his or her development) is directly proportional to the extent to which s/he was involved (both qualitatively and quantitatively).
- Academic performance is correlated with the student involvement.

This theory has many applications in the world of higher education and is one of the strongest pieces of evidence for co-curricular student involvement.

Researchers have continued to study this correlation with similar results. Student involvement in co-curricular activities such as student organizations, leadership positions, and activity in campus residence halls has a positive correlation with retention and academics (Kuh & Pike, 2005). Due to the positive aspects of co-curricular involvement, universities have been encouraging students to become involved.

If there is a criticism of Astin's (1993, 2000, 2013) theory, it is that it refers to behavior (what students do) rather than their feelings or thoughts. The latter may be more important when studying engagement, particularly in terms of feeling connected or committed to one's institution.

Sanford: Challenge and Support

Sanford (1966) contributed the notion of challenge and support to the field of student development. Two elements of this theory are specifically important to the consideration of engagement. The first is the cycle of differentiation and integration, as it relates to the process of development (Sanford, 1966). Students become differentiated when they see the unique aspects of their 'selves.' They become integrated when they are members of a group or community. Without the latter, students are not fully socially engaged in an institution.

Sanford (1966) proposed that students can become stymied developmentally if they do not have the academic, social or psychological skills, knowledge or attitude to weather the challenges that a campus can present. Without proper buffers to support them, they may disengage; thus, the amount of challenge any student can tolerate is directly related to his or her supports. The range of optimal dissonance for any particular student depends on the meaningfulness of the challenge and the degree of available support that a quality environment can provide. Without these, students may regress developmentally, ignore the challenge if escape is possible, or give up altogether.

Sanford (1966) believed that all students face some forms of challenge in college, but that these challenges vary for diverse populations. If the institutional environment is not set up to support different subpopulations through their challenges, or if students fail to experience supports that are there for them, they may be overwhelmed, unable to rise to the challenges or at risk for dropping out.

Schlossberg: Mattering and Marginality

Schlossberg's (1989) theory of 'mattering and marginality' is also inextricably linked to student engagement. As Patton et al., (2016) summarized

> *Feelings of marginality often occur when individuals take on new roles, especially when they are uncertain about what the new role entails. Schlossberg described marginality as a sense of not fitting in that can lead to self-consciousness, irritability, and depression. For members of minoritized groups, marginality is often a permanent condition; others, such as first-year students from dominant populations, may experience these feelings temporarily* (p. 36).

Feeling marginalized; therefore, leads a student to wonder if s/he matters to anyone on campus.

Schlossberg (1989) believed that there are four components of mattering. The first is attention, that is, the feeling of being noticed by others. The second is importance or believing that one is cared about by others. Ego-extension is defined as the feeling that someone else will be proud of the student's accomplishment or will empathize during a failure and, finally, dependence is the sense that others need the student. It is easy to see that advisors, faculty, peers, and other personnel such as coaches, mentors, or club leaders can provide these vital emotional connections to the campus. In their absence, a student is vulnerable to disengagement.

Schlossberg (1989) eventually added a fifth component of the model, that of appreciation of the student's efforts. These emotional states that comprise mattering are critical to empowering students to step into fully engaged social and academic roles at their institutions (Patton et al., 2016).

Rendon: Validation

A final theory that helps us understand college student engagement is that of validation. Rendon (1994) introduced this seminal concept through studies of both traditional and non-traditional college students. Traditional students, it was discovered, expressed few concerns that they would be academically successful, while non-traditional (who were defined as those from diverse racial, ethnic or cultural backgrounds) frequently doubted their ability to succeed (Rendon, 1994). These students became engaged in campus life only if they received forms of validation that bolstered their self-esteem and sense of self-efficacy. Rendon (1994) described validation as "an enabling, confirming and supportive process initiated by in-and out-of-class agents that foster academic and interpersonal development" (p. 46).

There were many environments in which the validation of college students might occur; these included the classroom, extracurricular activities, participation in campus organizations, social connections, or community experiences. The agents might be peers, faculty, residential staff, coaches, mentors, student services personnel, internship supervisors, or community service organizers, to name a few. What was important was that the agent was significant to the student in some manner (Rendon, 1994).

Validation is a process, not an end state, as the student could grow and extend in terms of his or her sense of worth and achievement (Rendon,

1994). The earlier the validation occurred, preferably in the first few weeks of being on campus, the greater the chance of its development. For those students who might experience imposter syndrome or self-doubt, early validation was even more important in the early experience of campus life (Davis, 2010).

Types of Student Engagement

Strayhorn: Sense of Belonging

Strayhorn (2012) saw a sense of belonging (one's social identity) as a fundamental human need, much in the same way that Maslow (1954) did. Strayhorn (2012), however, looked solely at its function within the field of college student engagement, defining a sense of belonging as

> *a basic human need and motivation, sufficient to influence behavior. In terms of college, a sense of belonging refers to students perceived social support on campus, a feeling or sensation of connectedness, the experience of mattering or feeling cared about, accepted, respected, valued by, and important to the group (e.g., campus community) or others on campus (e.g., faculty, peers* (p. 3).

Sense of belonging positively affects academic achievement, retention and persistence; conversely, students struggle to maintain academic engagement and commitment if they do not feel personally valued and welcome as a part of the campus community. At its worst, lack of sense of belonging can lead students to alienation, marginalization, disengagement, dropping out, depression or even suicidal thoughts.

Referencing Maslow's Hierarchy (1954), Strayhorn (2012) notes that belonging must occur before self-actualization in either cognitive or affective domains. Strayhorn (2012) categorizes the core elements of a sense of college student belonging. Belonging is a basic human need, strong enough to drive a student's behavior. This sense of belonging takes on heightened salience during different times and in different contexts in an individual's life; among these are times of transition and during the late adolescent/emerging adulthood quest for sense of autonomous self (Strayhorn, 2012). It also has heightened importance for individuals from populations on the social margins.

Sense of belonging in college is a consequence of what Strayhorn (2012) called 'mattering.' This feeling is reflected in the sense that it matters to others on campus whether the student shows up for class, persists to graduation, or is a valued member of campus groups or to his/her peers. An offshoot of this belief is that if one matters, s/he becomes valued to others and is more likely to try to preserve the bonds that matter through persistence, even through difficult times or tasks (Strayhorn, 2012). This is particularly true when a college student has close friends, mentors or faculty with whom s/he has bonded.

Social identities intersect and affect a student's sense of belonging. Strayhorn (2012) wrote that social identities are even more difficult for some students to construct because of the multiplicity of those identities; for example, an informant in the qualitative study of college students remarked:

> *Every part of me really shapes how I feel about belonging here (in college). It's not my Asian side saying 'Yes, I fit in here because I'm smart in science,' while the immigrant or working-class side of me says 'You're alone here, so go home'...it's actually all of them at once saying a combination of both things* (p. 22).

Among groups such as students of color, new immigrants, those with disabilities, and others who might be considered on the margins, Strayhorn (2012) found an emergent need to belong, to establish what he called "fictive kin"—family-like relationships with others on campus. This was intentional practice during summer bridge programs or other experiences that took place prior to matriculation, but it weakens after those take place. Students needed a continuous sense that there was "someone who would miss them if they didn't show up for class or left college entirely" (Strayhorn, 2012, p. 56).

Academic Engagement

In the classic, *Principles of Good Practice for Undergraduate Education,* Chickering & Gamson (1987) clearly articulated the categories of effective practice that have the greatest direct impact on student learning and the quality of their postsecondary learning experiences. Among these are cooperation between and among students, student-faculty interactions, time on task, prompt feedback, high academic expectations, active learning and a respect for the diversity of learners' styles and needs (Chickering & Gamson, 1987). In recent decades, the studies of effective andragogical practices have been at the heart of initiatives to promote college student success.

A great deal of influence has been placed on restructuring college learning environments to produce maximal student engagement in the learning process; much of this re-examination of teaching methods and learning theory comes as the result of the radical restructuring of the student body and its growing diversity. Results of these changes include setting higher academic standings, placing more responsibility on students for their own learning, adopting more active and collaborative methodologies, validating alternative ways of learning and demonstrating competency, and problem-focused learning (Kuh et al., 2006).

Sorcinelli (1991) wrote of the belief that if faculty demonstrated genuine regard for their students' unique interests and talents, they would be able to nurture student growth and development in all of the dominant spheres to include social, academic, emotional, personal and vocational. A student-success orientation at both the institutional and classroom level entails talent development as its primary focus, recognizing that all students can thrive under the right conditions and that institutions of higher learning have the ethical responsibility to provide those conditions.

Such a talent development philosophy is important for all students, yet it may be most critical for underserved populations as certain disciplines and courses are particularly challenging (Kuh et al., 2006). Beginning with the desire to learn what assets each student brings to the classroom, the instructor then creates ways for that student to share his or her unique perspective on the world and the topics under inquiry in a manner that enriches the learning of all in the classroom (Young, Celli, & Mumby, 2019).

Calculus and STEM courses are the most frequent among these. Rather than assuming that the students were unmotivated, disengaged, or incapable of succeeding, faculty at the University of Berkeley discovered that even though minority students had adequate backgrounds and abilities to succeed, they experienced environmental disorientation due to their learning style differences and often instructors' misinterpretation of these as academic deficiencies in need of remediation (Kuh et al., 2006). Starting with an unshakeable belief that the students could succeed, instructors set out to learn what kinds of learning environments best allowed the students to draw on preferred modes of learning to master and demonstrate mastery of the material.

Setting high expectations for all students and providing the support while holding them accountable for reaching these expectations is positively related to student academic success (Davis, 2009). Kuh et al. (2006) found that this single factor characterized schools that had higher than predicted student engagement and retention to graduation. Blose (1999) wrote that even students with poor prior academic history would rise to the higher expectations; yet, certain kinds of information and support are necessary to make this a reality.

Validation, "an enabling, confirming, and supportive process initiated by faculty and other agents of socialization in and out of the classroom---fosters student success, particularly for historically underserved students" (Kuh, Kinzie, Schuh, & Whitt, 2005a, p. 67). Validation involves such activities as referring to students by name, encouraging students to collaborate, support and validate each other, working individually with students, and providing praise for their efforts. These are the activities that can be transformative in teaching and learning and they increase students' engagement, even when the work is difficult.

Studies on effective classroom approaches concur that active learning, classrooms in which students are intellectually challenged, learning new and meaningful things, and are able to relate both to the instructor and peers are places where engaged scholarship takes place (Braxton, Milem, & Sullivan, 2000). What mattered in the learning process of historically underserved students was that they could learn with others, have chances to take part in active learning such as research projects, group projects or presentations, and have opportunities to engage in lots of discussion with classmates.

Braxton et al. (2000) found that active and collaborative learning is correlated with increased engagement and social integration, institutional commitment, and intent to persist at an institution. Such classroom experiences are positively related to increased student contact with both faculty and peers because of the nature of learning assignments and with more positive views of the campus in general, most likely because of greater interaction with classmates.

Interestingly, instructional technology was cited by students as having a salutary effect on their academic engagement (Kuh et al., 2005a). If students used information technology often in their assignments or used social media to discuss coursework with peers, they reported feeling more engaged in their classes and with their faculty. They also participated more often with other classmates outside of the classroom if their faculty encouraged the use of instructional technology. Students from low-SES groups, as well as adults who held jobs and first-generation college students reported their appreciation for online materials because those helped them balance life and college responsibilities. Students who might otherwise have been hesitant to contribute orally in classroom settings were more likely to do so as part of posts or discussion boards if those activities were required in online classes (Kuh et al., 2005a).

Weimer (2012) reported on principles of engaged teaching that should result in the same type of learning. Faculty first needs to enhance their students' self-belief, especially among new and/or fragile student populations (Weimer, 2012). Students' beliefs about themselves as learners and their ability to engage when they act as their own agents of learning, ensure that their efforts towards goals that are personally meaningful are obtained. They must hold the belief that they can learn, even in the face of challenging assignments, and that they can use academic failures to further their learning (Weimer, 2012). Faculty serve as powerful agents in that they can both give students some control over their learning processes and can act as encouragers, prompting them to have faith in their abilities.

Another principle involves giving students different types of learning opportunities. They need both chances to operate as autonomous learners, as well as learning how to cooperate with others in collaborative learning projects (Zepke & Leach, 2010). Learning with peers, in groups, in mentored study with faculty bolsters both social skills and academic ones. Mastering all of these situations feeds a sense of self-efficacy (Hsieh, Sullivan, & Guerra, 2007).

Faculty are at the heart of the engagement process and when perceived as "approachable, well prepared, and sensitive to student needs, students are committed to work harder, get more out of the session, and are more willing to express their opinion" (Zepke & Leach, 2010, p. 170). These students are more willing to engage if their educational experiences are challenging and enriching and stretch them beyond their current level of academic ability. Rich experiences in the classroom are those that require students to reflect, ask questions, pose conjectures, evaluate, and make connections among ideas.

Ten Considerations for Better Learning

Kytle (2004) tackled the task of defining the conditions for engaged learning on college campuses. The first condition stated that learning needs a purpose. Learning communities must have clear purposes, values, and norms that are evident in every facet of college life; beyond that "the mission must be alive in the entire institution" (Kytle, 2004, p. 129). The clear mission will, by its very nature, help students and faculty self-select because they want to learn in a particular ethos.

Engaged learning, Kytle (2004) stated, also needs individualization. All meaningful human learning is individualized, which is not a radical idea "until we think about the ways schools and colleges are organized so as to violate that order" (Kytle, 2004, p. 130). Faculty must create time and space for their students to ponder the questions of the life-project such as 'Who am I?,' 'Where am I going?,' and 'Why?' Like many other theorists and practitioners, Kytle (2004) promotes the incorporating journals, diaries, and writing assignments that ask students to synthesize personal experience with the academic content of their courses, the integration of theory and praxis reflective assignments, and the formulation of individual theories of best practice. An authentic, engaged existence entails the ability to be an effective member of a team, as well as a contributing member of one's community and the society as a whole (Kytle, 2004).

Engaged learning additionally requires 'predicaments.' A good curriculum "probes and challenges the human spirit—it is not a set of courses, a collection of professors, or a degree earned...Good learning settings test character traits, perseverance, and organizational skills" (Kytle, 2004, p. 133). Learners should be involved in struggling to make better questions rather than the right answers for standardized exams. Kytle (2004) believed that writing should be our national obsession, as it does a far better job of engaging students and stimulating critical thinking than do standardized exams.

Another key consideration is that learners need mentors (Whitebook & Bellum, 2014). In the author's definition, faculty and staff who serve as student mentors must be an embodiment of the engaged life themselves as they must be able to be life coaches as well (Kytle, 2004; Whitebook & Bellum, 2014).

Another consideration is that learning is most likely to occur in what Kuh et al. (1991) described as small spaces, human places. The psychological size of a campus may be far different from its actual physical or quantitative number of students. Psychological size matters; large institutions can create human places by breaking themselves down into smaller communities in which students are known and cared about and where they feel safe (Kytle, 2004). As Kytle (2004) puts it, "small schools let teachers know a student by name, letting them recognize subtle changes in mood or a different learning style" (p. 141). Empirical studies have supported that learning communities create engagement and if students experience a campus as smaller in psychological size, a campus can exert a more powerful influence educationally, as it permits students a closer view of the life of the mind and how to participate in that life (Pascarella & Terenzini, 1991).

Another consideration Kytle (2004) mentions is that learning needs process before content. Colleges and universities, the author opines, must promote the learning process, per se, rather than focusing solely on disciplinary content. While there definitely are essential bodies of knowledge that form the basis for mastery of a particular discipline or professional practice, the most valuable kinds of learning are the processes that can be used throughout one's lifetime and have utility across multiple situations and (Kytle, 2004). Cooperative, self-directed courses and work-study type programs typify this kind of learning.

Learners also need two types of experiences; reflective experience in class and timely feedback (Kytle, 2004; Galindo, 2018). The former may take the shape of a variety of classroom surveys and also might include student written narrative evaluations of their work that they share with their instructors. Feedback, in order to be effective, needs to be timely, balanced, directional (suggesting what needs improving), holistic and detailed (Galindo, 2018). Formative feedback is the most valuable to the student (Kytle, 2004).

Learning needs theory is the formulation of mental models that help students "because they carry purposes and justifications needed to motivate new investments of scarce time and energy" (Kytle, 2004, p. 155). Students need to learn about their own ways of learning as their faculty must do (Kytle, 2004). Learning to examine our thinking as we are doing it requires a different kind of faculty and mentor relationship he says. Kytle (2004) suggests that all students explicate a life-project before they begin their studies, describing "their dreams, deepest values, and life purposes" (p. 156); this forms the basis of a dialogue between student and advisor/mentor throughout the whole program of study and is imbedded in several of the approaches described in the chapter on advancing academic advising.

Social and Extracurricular Engagement

While most discussions of college student engagement harken back to Tinto's (1993) theory, there is concern that little empirical evidence exists to support it, yet almost everyone agrees that in order to experience success in college, students must be able to navigate new environments, transitions, and social situations. Social networks are the psychological safety net that can buffer students in times of crisis (Pescosolido, 1994).

Social networks of like-minded peers can consolidate behavioral repertoires and lead to engaged action—either positive or negative (Wertalik, 2017). Some students are too burdened with other commitments to build these social networks and thus are likely to be less connected to their campus. To reach these students with greater extra-college life commitments, institutions must carefully plan appropriate activities that work around barriers.

The National Survey of Student Engagement (2018) revealed the inextricable link between taking part in a variety of social and extracurricular activities and a student's level of overall engagement. Webber, Krylow & Zhang (2013) note that taking part in more academic and extracurricular activities positively correlated with higher cumulative GPAs and students' rating of their academic experience as a whole. There are particular kinds of activities that boost student engagement and colleges should host these regularly because student participation in them improves their social and academic achievements such as community service days, assignments that promote collaboration among students, faculty-student interactions outside of the classroom, campus speakers, intramural sports, learning communities, creative projects, and opportunities for research (Webber et al., 2013).

A fascinating concept referred to as the psychological size of a campus proposes that a student's degree of social integration within an institution has less to do with the campus' absolute size and more to do with how connected a student is to social networks within the larger community (Webber et al., 2013). Factors contributing to this kind of size include

> *the formation of peer groups, on-campus residential facilities, high-quality advising, and small-group instruction. A larger campus can feel smaller and more personal when students have available (and take advantage of) activities such as first-year learning groups arranged by academic discipline or interest topic, common reading activities that bring students and faculty together for discussion, Facebook or Second Life islands for students at the institution, intramural sports arranged by academic major or residency hall, and/or residency hall floor meetings with faculty speakers that encourage dialogue between faculty and students in a more relaxed setting outside the classroom* (Webber et al., 2013, p.608).

These activities should continue throughout all years of enrollment, not just the first-year experience.

Final Thoughts

What happens once a student matriculates in college is the most powerful factor in shaping his or her engagement, bond to the college or university, and persistence to graduation. The National Survey of Student Engagement (2018), which now has collected data from approximately four million undergraduate students in this country, has identified practices that have a powerful impact on student engagement. Among these are academic challenge, learning with peers, experiences with faculty and the campus environment. There also are high-impact practices that are impactful. These include service learning, study abroad, being able to conduct research with faculty, and internships.

Student engagement in the aforementioned practices is defined as educationally purposeful; it leads to deep levels of learning and produces positive outcomes across a number of domains, including cognitive, emotional, psychological and social. But how these practices are constructed and offered may be different on each campus. There is no 'one size fits all' approach to student engagement. All prominent researchers and authors on this topic agree that the responsibility for student engagement crosses all offices on campus and is shared between students and institutional representatives. Colleges and universities cannot apply magical thinking, believing that simply because they make opportunities available, all students will engage.

Points to Remember

- *Students' experiences in college after they have matriculated are more important in shaping their engagement, connection to the institution, and persistence to graduation than any factors that occur prior to matriculation.*
- *College student engagement maybe defined as the amount of time and effort students put into their studies and other educationally purposeful practices, in and outside of the classroom.*
- *A second component of student engagement is how the institution allocates resources and organizes its learning experiences and support services to induce students to take part in the educationally purposeful practices.*
- *Engagement leads to positive gains, benefits and outcomes in cognitive, moral, social, career and psychological domains.*
- *Engagement in one's studies and the life of the college are positively linked to higher GPAs and greater likelihood of persistence to graduation.*
- *There are both social and academic spheres of student engagement.*
- *Engagement engenders a sense of belonging and commitment to an institution of higher learning.*

Chapter Two

Student and Campus Challenges: Contemporary Solutions to Engagement

Engaging college students is no easy task as there are as many reasons to deviate from studies as there are to persist. College professors face the online learning curve, as much in creating an online presence as focusing students who are digital natives and adept at multitasking online. It becomes necessary, then, to use a multitude of strategies to attract and interest Generation Z students and their older, more mature, contemporary peers.

Self-learning, or personalized learning, connects concepts to real-world applications and offers the student a way to immediately use the information learned. A collaborative mentality between professor and learner paves the way for interesting and valuable class time, while understanding student learning styles is also an important ingredient. Providing students with clear assignments and syllabi, as well as interesting and meaningful assignments will also help curb any issues. Students value internships and opportunities to have hands-on experiences; thus, it becomes necessary to eliminate any barriers to these activities.

Online Learning

Online learning presents faculty with new challenges that they have not encountered in traditional classrooms due to student separation from their instructors by computer screens. This requires faculty to develop different engagement strategies for all aspects of course design-- content, learning activities, and assessments (Young, Jean, & Quayson, 2017). New technologies also create new social challenges, as instructors confront questions of how to prevent feelings of frustration or isolation and how best to keep students at a distance highly-motivated (Briggs, 2015).

While barriers that contemporary faculty face in online teaching exist, there are strategies to overcome them. In the social domain, there is a need to build a strong community in online courses. Interaction with both faculty and peers is key to engagement; thus, the professor should make contact before the course actually begins; create community-building introductory activities to build a community of scholars; provide discussion opportunities for learner interaction, create online study groups; and encourage sharing through social media (Briggs, 2015).

There are potential administrative barriers that can reduce engagement; for example, students may get frustrated if they don't know how and when to contact instructors or they may become discouraged if they are not able to keep abreast of their progress in the course or if expectations aren't clearly communicated (Briggs, 2015). Establishing contact methods and hours at the very beginning of the course and holding online office hours provides a clear way for students to communicate. Briggs (2015) also reminds instructors that directions and expectations need to be conveyed in multiple ways. Timely and meaningful feedback is a key to engagement in any academic setting, so it is equally important online (Young, Jean, & Quayson, 2017).

Briggs (2015) remarks that there are also motivational barriers that can become an impediment to online engagement. This may be even more prevalent if students are trying to engage in coursework in settings that have built-in distractions such as home or office. Chunking course content in smaller segments and using a wide variety of modalities to deliver that content are two effective strategies (Briggs, 2015). So are reminders and checklists so that students can track progress towards deadlines, as are video or phone conferences with students who are falling off track.

Pearson (2018) developed a differentiated curriculum to augment its texts; yet, they posit that many faculties simply need to retool their teaching strategies to combine the best of all methodologies. Teaching in an outdated "one size fits all" mentality that still relies heavily on lectures (and often outdated class resources) will be a definite turnoff for new millennials and other learners who are used to new technology (Pearson, 2018). Faculty must be urged to invest time and energy in retooling their materials and methodologies (Young, Jean, & Quayson, 2017).

Engaging Diverse Student Populations

As campuses become more complex, they must move from what Quaye & Harper (2015) call the 'magical thinking' that often defines practices of student engagement to intentionality. Simply providing services for students is not enough to enhance their educational experience and naively expecting that if students of diverse backgrounds come into contact with each other on campus, they will share their views, identities and experiences and learn from one another is not sufficient. Rather, it behooves instructors to

> *facilitate structured opportunities for these dialogues to transpire. Meaningful strategies are necessary that enable institutions to realize the benefits of engaging diverse populations... When an institution provides reinforcements for students, it means educators have envisioned and enacted the types of learning opportunities that will contribute to student development and engagement* (Quaye & Harper, 2015, p. 7).

Before these strategies can be developed and implemented, all college personnel involved in student engagement strategies must first understand the barriers to full engagement, as defined and perceived by students on the margins (Quaye & Harper, 2015). Deliberate practice rests on a deep understanding of the life-worlds of those students who are not fully engaged in educationally purposeful activities. This requires listening to such students, inviting those who are least engaged, or most likely to be marginalized to share their stories (Quaye & Harper, 2015). Without qualitative input and actual involvement from these populations, strategies may be ill-founded.

Strategies for Engaging Generation Z

Wondergem (2017) proposes that Generation Z, whose oldest members are now 21, will provide a new challenge for college engagement, given that they have grown up without a memory of a world without technology. They are poised to be stellar college students, if teaching is adapted to their needs, because they are self-learners and rapid information processors (Wondergem, 2017).

These students will arrive on college campuses with some unique characteristics. Among them is the overreliance on technology and round-the-clock access to any information that they need. They also have an "8 second attention filter," (Wondergem, 2017, p. 3) requiring immediate responses. Wondergem (2017) also points out that the "average Gen Z learner can multitask across 5 devices at a time" (p. 3). Effective teaching strategies involve not only technology use and the "flipped" classroom but connecting classroom content to real-world applications to problem-solving (Young, Jean, & Quayson, 2017).

Gen Z learners tend to see issues from global perspectives and can be influenced by peer opinion, as well as taking a "big picture" approach to problem-solving (Wondergem, 2017). This generation of student has no problem accessing information but need critical thinking skills to determine if sources are credible (The Center for generational Kinetics, 2017). Information literacy lies behind all classroom teaching, as does synthesis of the vast amounts of material that may be easily found.

Because Gen Z students are able to utilize their social contacts in ways that make them learning tools, it can be argued that they are participating in learning essentially non-stop (Wondergem, 2017). If these tools are employed, students are less likely to be passive learners as they enjoy sharing the knowledge that they have created in public forums. The learning experience has primacy; engaging these students without compromising academic content requires some skill (Wondergem, 2017).

One suggestion is to allow Gen Z students to use technology and take advantage of their drive for self-learning by incorporating devices into learning activities while, at the same time, teaching them how to assess the credibility of sources and information (Wondergem, 2017). Second, faculty is urged to build a social network beyond the classroom by being available through social apps for questions or clarifications (Wondergem, 2017). Connecting classroom materials to student relevance as well as global problems and solutions is also integral, as is providing quick feedback. Finally, the instructor should use far less of the 'sage on the stage' approach and instead provide brief, visual presentations chunked into microlessons to pique student interest and engagement (Wondergem, 2017).

Implications for Colleges and Universities

Strayhorn (2012) reports on specific practices that institutions do to engender a sense of belonging on campus. These begin with connecting students to others with similar interests, values, and goals in an intentional fashion (Strayhorn, 2012). They also make sure that students are familiar with the campus environment and ecology prior to beginning their actual studies. This may take place in pre-college experiences and also in orientations, courses (both credit and non-credit bearing) and living/learning communities. In addition, students who were engaged in and committed to their college communities felt that they mattered and that others depended on them (Strayhorn, 2012).

In 2006, Kuh et al. published one of the most extensive studies of the literature on college student success. In understanding why, this study centered on student engagement, the authors cited their belief that it represented

> aspects of student behavior and institutional performance that colleges and universities can do something about, at least on the margins, whereas many other factors such as precollege characteristics are typically beyond the direct control of the student or the college or university.
> (Kuh et al., 2006, p. 3)

High levels of student engagement are associated with a wide range of institutional practices and contexts that relate to student persistence, satisfaction, educational achievement and whole-student development (Kuh et al., 2006).

The National Student Engagement Survey (2018) involved 650 colleges and universities in the United States and 72 in Canada. Among the findings were those relating to inclusive teaching practices, intentional diversity-related programming, and the perception that one's college environment was truly welcoming and supportive of all students (National Student Engagement Survey, 2018). When those conditions were met, students were able to engage with their studies in a way that bolstered their higher order learning, sense of belonging, and intercultural competence. Students who reported more inclusive classroom practices also perceived greater personal and social gains, as well as becoming more active and informed citizens (National Student Engagement Survey, 2018).

First-generation students were more likely not to take part or be able to take part in the identified high-impact practices; however, gaps between their participation and that of others were smaller as they persisted (National Student Engagement Survey, 2018). Much of the gap seems to be related to lack of knowledge of these opportunities, so that first-generation students were less likely to plan to seek them out. The implication for institutions is that their roles must include being effective disseminators of the information that students need and must do this extremely early on in these students' first year (or before) and work to eliminate financial barriers and other impediments for those from low-income backgrounds (National Student Engagement Survey, 2018).

The 2017 survey included revamped questions aimed at studying gender identity, sexual orientation, and student engagement (National Student Engagement Survey, 2018). Gender variant students were more likely than their cisgender peers to feel personally supported on college campuses in terms of general wellbeing and help with managing non-academic responsibilities (National Student Engagement Survey, 2018). Student services and administrative staff and offices were most often mentioned as sources of discontent; however, gender variant students were more apt to be student leaders or were involved in original research projects with their faculty members (National Student Engagement Survey, 2018).

The survey also found that LGBQ+ students were more engaged than cisgender peers in learning activities that were reflective, integrative, or connected learning to societal problems (National Student Engagement Survey, 2018). Student engagement and persistence also was influenced by the perceived quality of student-faculty interactions as most first-year students expected to have frequent interactions with faculty; the substance of these exchanges may include career plans, coursework, or other activities such as clubs, internships, or research (National Student Engagement Survey, 2018). If there is a gap between expectations and actuality, students are more likely to disengage.

The study recognizes the fact that many entering students may have unrealistic expectations or may not know how to initiate the kinds of interactions that they desire (National Student Engagement Survey, 2018). Institutions must address these issues in orientation or first-year programs to avoid student disappointment and disengagement; faculty also need to be apprised of student expectations so that they can help students with setting realistic expectations for their interactions.

One question raised in this year's survey was whether there is a link between student activism and engagement to which the answer seems to be positive (National Student Engagement Survey, 2018). Rather than fearing or trying to suppress student activism, the study argues, institutions should embrace it because those who are engaged in campus activism and governance are more likely to emphasize higher order learning (National Student Engagement Survey, 2018). Some of the positive outcomes of such engagement are exposure to greater diversity, the ability to consider others' points of views, reassessing one's own beliefs, and other critical thinking skills.

While the most recent National Survey of Student Engagement (2018) indicated that, increasingly, colleges and universities are making student engagement a greater priority, it found that most are not reaping much in the way of benefits in engagement and retention overall. Institutions, therefore, need to invite new participants to the engagement conversation (Robsham, 2016). There are a number of campus groups who are typically excluded but need to be brought into efforts to include dining services; operations and facilities; administrative personnel; students who have demonstrated engagement; and successful graduates (Robsham, 2016).

There are simple yet impactful steps that lead to inclusiveness such as scouring all institutional communication with students to personalize and/or use gender inclusive words. Greater staff and faculty training in professional interactions with marginalized groups, as well as the "mobile first generation" also are valuable. Robsham (2016) suggests having faculty and staff partner with admissions and enrollment management for sessions in which those staff have pulled major "themes" from application essays, illuminating students' dreams, hopes, and fears, thus humanizing each incoming class. Demographic information about the percentages who self-identify as first generation, disabled, or different ethnic groups helps the college prepare for each unique entering class (Robsham, 2016).

There are generational gaps between faculty/staff and college students, with each newly entering class having its own life trajectory; for example, The Mindset List (2018) reminds us that the class of 2019 has never licked a stamp; has always had hybrid automobiles; and was recorded by their parents with camcorders!

Robsham (2016) views one of the most divisive aspects of campus life as the silo mentality, which is described as departments or academic units communicating amongst themselves solely rather than having big picture institutional goals at the forefront of any discussion or planning. In order to have successful student engagement initiatives, a culture of collaboration must be developed, with different units describing their goals and proposed activities, and the group buying into a set of institution and division-wide strategies that represent shareable ground for all (Robsham, 2016).

Institutions can also address some common barriers to student engagement. Among these are actions that deter students from getting involved because they waste time and cause frustration (Quality Assurance Agency, 2012). These include multiple websites with the same information, loading students with too much information, requiring multiple unnecessary logins, or having to go from office to office in an attempt to find paper forms or information that is required. Paperwork, by and large, is frequently lost, misplaced, or forgotten. Robsham (2016) urges institutions to use electronic forms and set up efficient workflows, cross train office personnel, streamline online processes, and adopt engagement software.

Nygaard et al. (2013), in a study of student engagement in the United Kingdom, found that involving students as practitioner partners raised their level of investment. This included hiring students in professional roles, providing internships, and building student advisory boards. The increased level of student participation, recognition of student voice, and student involvement in shaping their own learning experiences led to higher levels of engagement and achievement (Nygaard et al., 2013).

Participants were asked to reflect on what had mattered in their learning development and increased ownership and this brought the realization that there were common themes regarding student engagement (Nygaard et al., 2013). Among these were

- students' ability to find their own learning styles and be able to articulate them to others,
- the use of healthy competitiveness as a basis for student motivation,
- being positively influenced by inspirational, passionate "wacky" professors who clearly loved their subject matter and inspired the students to do the same,
- time management and organizational skills were instrumental, as was recognizing prior life experience,
- working in groups, having positive role models, and learning with gangs of friends,
- a better work ethic when it was felt that someone believed in the learner.

This last point echoed Terenzini et al.'s (1994) concept that students will work hard for faculty with whom they have formed a powerful bond so that they will not fall short of their faculty's expectations of them.

Mansfield University, Pennsylvania (2012) developed retention efforts that were built around twelve best practices for student engagement. These included the recognition that so many first-year students arrive on campus "adrift" and need structure to be successful during their transition. Falling behind by even a few assignments can be cause for failure so it is essential that there be an early warning and tracking system, including a mandatory class attendance policy, for all first-year students and those in lower-level classes (Mansfield University, 2012).

There also needed to be early contact with advisors—within the first two weeks or earlier—that again is mandatory; some departments or advisee groups may have mandatory socials at the start of the year to encourage connections (Mansfield University, 2012).

Tinto (2012) stressed that academic and social engagement must begin in each class in the very first session and that devoting the initial class meeting to the kinds of activities that excite the students about the syllabus and course materials, helping them find personal connections to the material and learning objectives increased engagement overall. Activities that help students get to know their classmates so that they can partner in the learning process is another helpful tool. Rather than handing students a syllabus and dismissing class, faculty should create an engaged classroom learning community from day one (Mansfield University, 2012).

Another role that faculty and staff can play in initial meetings is to help students find connection points through engaging with even one campus activity, club, or community group (Mansfield University, 2012). This has been linked with persistence to graduation. Goal-setting also is related to engagement, as students with clear academic, career and personal goals are more engaged in their education; goal-setting activities that link to career-planning guidance can be incorporated into classroom activities and advising sessions (Tinto, 2012).

While much attention is paid to first-year activities, advisors should duplicate these efforts with returning second and third-year students as well. Providing academic check-ups at the very beginning of those years can ensure that students are on track to graduation and are invested in the academic concentrations and extracurricular activities that keep them engaged (Mansfield University, 2012).

There are a variety of recommended techniques to actively engage students in their classrooms, particularly as they learn the ropes of college coursework in their first-year classes and seminars. These involve active learning that springs from problem-focused discussions, group work, and the use of stimulating technology. Writing, even in small amounts, is a productive class exercise. Techniques such as the one-minute paper, weekly journals, reflective writing assignments, and activities that require students to write about campus events they have attended all build class engagement and communication between students and faculty and among their peers (Mansfield University, 2012).

Mansfield University (2012) suggests the maxim of test early/test often although by 'test' it is clear that we are talking about multiple kinds of assessment. The main point is to make sure that students demonstrate their learning on a regular basis and that instructors can note and remediate problems before they become so overwhelming that students disengage (Mansfield University, 2012). The concept of mid-term and final assessments is completely outdated with current emphasis on formative evaluation using multiple methods of demonstrating knowledge. Faculty can also build supplemental instruction or course-centered study groups into their courses, assigning points for participation (Mansfield University, 2012). Overall, there are many powerful student engagement techniques available to faculty (Barkley, 2010).

How to Get the Most Out of College

The nation's obsession with getting adolescents into college is equal to the silence on how to "navigate the crucial college years to best effect. It's strange. And it's stupid, because how a student goes to college matters much, much more than where" (Bruni, 2018, p. 1). Bruni (2018) says that the focus of his years of "gathering wisdom" while on college campuses leads him to his "focus on optimal ways to socialize, to prioritize, to pick up skills integral to any career and to open up exciting possibilities both en route to a degree and after you've acquired it" (p. 6). What Bruni (2018) is describing fits the definition of student engagement.

Bruni (2018) further goes on to point out that the wisest students "move into a peer relationship with the institution rather than a consumer relationship" (p. 6). Such students also take on leadership roles, build social capital, and widen their circle of friends and mentors. Rather than isolating themselves in relationships with those like themselves, with whom they feel most comfortable, they branch out into a more diverse network (Bruni, 2018). A level of comfort in diverse situations certainly serves one well in any profession or field.

As part of the research, Bruni (2018) also asked past winners of the Mitchell scholarship to reflect on what elements of college were most important to them and not surprisingly, relationships with faculty topped the list. These faculty were able to act as bridges to other influential people, both on and off campus, and opened many doors for their students. This led to scholarships, travel abroad, research opportunities and special programs, as well as better internships and recommendations for graduate work (Bruni, 2018).

Bruni (2018) cites the Strada-Gallup Alumni Survey (over 100,000 graduates of American colleges), that shows that there is not a correlation between a student's engagement in and satisfaction with his or her higher education experiences and attendance at "prestigious" institutions. The critical factors, the survey found, overwhelmingly are that the student makes deep connections with others, experiences mentorship, plays a role in a club, team or service activity, and takes part in at least one ongoing academic project (Bruni, 2018). Another element is finding

> what lies closest to your heart...If you are fortunate enough to find something that you're totally obsessed with, you're likely to work very hard at it. If you're a human being of average intelligence and you work very hard at it, you're likely to become very good at it. And if you become very good at it, people are likely to notice

(James Gates of Brown University, as cited in Bruni, 2018, p. 7).

As a final note, Wiley (2018) touts the symbiotic benefits of student engagement for both students and institutions. Wiley (2018) disagrees with the narrow view of student engagement as institutionally beneficial "in terms of how best to leverage the channels of engagement—email, text messages, social media, etc.—for recruitment and alumni gift giving" (p. 1). Instead, it should be considered as "a robust path for providing a better student experience, increasing students' sense of belonging, driving better student achievement, or enhancing the reputation of their institution" (Wiley, 2018, p. 1). Engagement, when executed correctly, benefits students across their lifespan; however, the crux is in what key relationships it genuinely promotes, and those relationships can be student/institutional mission, student/student, student/faculty and advisors, or student/learning activities (Wiley, 2018).

What Wiley (2018) terms 'truly robust student engagement' relies on three stances. The first is to focus on the student viewpoint, understanding what engagement means from a student's eye view. The only way to determine this viewpoint is to ask. Second is the breaking down of silo mentality and expanding the list of players in any engagement initiative. Third is overcoming a reliance on technology, which Wiley (2018) says some institutions see as the silver bullet in enhanced engagement. While it certainly has its place, it is not the be all and end all in all situations.

Students benefit significantly, Wiley (2018) found, by belonging to a community, yet this is not necessarily a natural occurrence in college life. Institutions must think of engagement strategies in terms of all students, especially those for whom college may be a culture shock and those who exist on the margins of many campuses. Improved student achievement can flow from engagement, both engagement with course content and within stimulating learning environments, such as learning groups, living/learning communities, or faculty collaborations in research or service learning (Wiley, 2018).

The benefits for institutions fall into two categories. The first relates to improved retention rates, especially for specific groups who may arrive on campus struggling to adapt to its demands. These include first-year, adult learners, low-income, first-generation, minority group members, military veterans, and underprepared students, to name a few (Engle & Tinto, 2008; Young, Michael, & Jean, 2019). Alumni offices may also see benefits in increased alumni involvement and giving if they perceive a deep connection to their alma mater, rather than feeling that it provided them only with a degree, rather than a transformative life experience.

Final Thoughts

Ensuring that students can access the academics using collaborative means, online learning that is easy to use and comprehend, professors who probe students to understand learning styles, providing internships and meaningful hands-on experiences, as well as personalized learning opportunities, all encourage engagement and limit or eliminate barriers to learning.

There are particular groups of students who are more able and comfortable taking part in engagement opportunities. The challenge for each institution is to determine groups on the margins and make special efforts to program with their interests and needs in mind. One way to improve practice is to invite members of these populations to discussions that inform programming in order to hear diverse students' experiences and suggestions for improved opportunities.

Knowing that students who have not formed meaningful relationships with peers and faculty and who may not be familiar or comfortable with office, organizations, or groups on campus are at far greater risk of disengaging or dropping out altogether. Quaye & Harper (2015) sum up the process of arriving at a captivating campus with these words

> *Creating optimal learning environments in which all students feel connected is difficult, but nonetheless important. Educators must have the requisite skills and expertise to analyze the campus environment and determine where gaps in engagement and achievement exist. More importantly, they must resist the urge to act without considering the effects of potential solutions and instead, spend time understanding the obstacles facing disengaged students* (p. 7).

Points to Remember

- *It is vital to create an online learning platform that is easy to use and understand. Assignments must be clear, interesting, and meaningful.*
- *Personalized learning opportunities to include online and internships support students and limit or eliminate barriers to education.*
- *Particular student subpopulations, such as women, those who live on campus, those taking part in field experiences, those who participate in clubs and organizations, or those*

who start and finish at the same institution have greater connection to their campuses.
- *Faculty and staff play critical roles in creating experiences and relationships that lead to student engagement on campus.*
- *There are symbiotic benefits to both students and institutions as a result of meaningful engagement initiatives.*
- *The most impactful campus practices all are active in nature: being a part of a learning community; engaging in research with faculty; having an opportunity to study abroad or take part in internship experiences; being a member of a club, team or service organization; and being part of a learning project that unfolds over time.*
- *In order to create effective engagement initiatives, more players need to be invited into the discussion, including disengaged students.*

Chapter Three

Preparation for Postsecondary Success: Promoting Positive Campus Transitions

There are many types of programs that can help students transition from high school to a prosperous and successful college career. Successful programs assist new students in making a smooth transition into college and gain the attitudes, knowledge, skills, and opportunities that will allow them to be engaged and productive members of the collegiate community (Hibel & Hernandez, 2018).

Like many programs, they are not one size fits all. Colleges and universities should take care to conduct a thorough review of profiles of new students to determine what their assets, needs and challenges might be; they then can use this information to compare them to the mission, values and goals of their institution (Hibel & Hernandez, 2018). Once these things have been considered, it is only then that institutions can discern the appropriate pieces of information new students will require in order to fully integrate academically and socially to the institution (Hibel & Hernandez, 2018).

Summer Bridge Programs

For many recent secondary school graduates, summer bridge programs ease their way onto campus by providing students with the requisite academic and social skills for success in a college environment (U.S. Department of Education, 2016). These college readiness programs typically take place in the period between high school and the start of college and although the content of programs will vary, they typically last 2–4 weeks and involve an in-depth orientation to life at college including resources, academic advising, and training in college success skills such as time management and study skills, and/or accelerated academic coursework (U.S. Department of Education, 2016).

Although summer bridge programs have been historically targeted toward ethnic/racial minority, low-income, first-generation, or other at-risk populations, they are now being used for all general education students (U.S. Department of Education, 2016). For general education students, the goal is to provide academic support that prepares students for college-level work and helps them navigate the transition to college by giving them general information about college life and resources (U.S. Department of Education, 2016). Nonacademic college readiness components of summer bridge programs are designed to provide cultural and social resources to students and promote adjustment to college culture (U.S. Department of Education, 2016).

Creating Effective Bridge Programs

Numerous colleges have invested in bridge programs to help promising borderline students adjust to college-level work; however, many of these programs fail to actually support student success as they focus on non-credit-bearing courses and/or undermine student confidence by singling them out as needing special help (Silverman, 2017).

Effective bridge programs are guided by principles that focus on core classes, encourage an early start on Pell funding, and specifically communicate in a way that frames bridge programs as positive opportunities (Silverman, 2017). For those students that are admitted conditionally, they end up starting after the rest of their incoming class and are forced to take remedial classes, which can put them at least a year behind in starting credit-bearing coursework (Silverman, 2017).

Post-secondary institutions should consider inviting academically at-risk students to skip remediation entirely and start college-level coursework the summer before their official freshman fall semester (Silverman, 2017). Students can enroll as a unified cohort in classes already offered during the summer alongside upperclassman who serve as models of college success. As a cohort, students can attend financial counseling, advising, tutoring, and supplemental instruction to ensure they are prepared to succeed in college-level classes (Silverman, 2017).

Student Orientation

The first opportunity that a college or university has to inculcate its culture, values and mission into first-year students is its orientation program. Here, students gain critical information about expectations and opportunities, resources and cultural norms (Ready Education, 2016). It also marks the beginning of exposure to the social community of all new learners and can be a wonderful setting for forming lasting connections. Social involvement activities at orientation provide incoming students with the chance to interact with orientation leaders and current students through icebreakers, student panels, or engaging with student clubs (Ready Education, 2016). Some of the most effective events include inviting veteran students from a variety of clubs and organizations to talk about their first-year college experiences, sharing tips for success and answering questions. Student engagement fairs where newcomers could learn about campus resources and activities also ease the transition (Ready Education, 2016).

To get students engaged and connected early on, college campuses should instill a sense of college pride in new students by displaying the school mascot and giving out free college gear (Ready Education, 2016). Taking students' photos and posting them using the college's social media accounts familiarizes students with those platforms and increases interest in becoming users (Ready Education, 2016).

During orientation, it is imperative that new students and their families feel supported (Shupp, 2014). Acclimating to college life can be a confusing and stressful experience and college staff should not assume that students, particularly first generations students, can navigate the beginning of college on their own. Orientations should aim to make processes as simple and efficient as possible with all available resources and individuals on deck to answer questions and provide additional support (Ready Education, 2016). Students, for example, might be given their class schedule at orientation, meet their advisor, or speak with a financial aid counselor about the loan process.

Social Media

Students who have graduated high school are often left feeling lost and overwhelmed with what needs to happen in the transition to college (Coles, 2015). To assist in the summer transition, some colleges and universities turn to social media and text messaging. One university sent their incoming students a series of text messages regarding the steps that would need to be completed before entering college including information on placement tests, freshman orientation, the deadline for paying their tuition bill, and how to accept their loans (Ahlquist, 2014; Boucher, 2014). Another group of students at the same college were matched with local peer advisors who conducted outreach activities via phone, e-mail, Facebook, and texting to arrange in-person meetings in which the mentors provided students with the information and assistance to complete the tasks to transition to college (Boucher, 2014; Coles, 2015). Both of these practices resulted in an increased number of students starting college, with text messaging having the greatest impact in communities where students had less access to college planning assistance (Ahlquist, 2014; Coles, 2015).

Connect with a Student Leader

First year students should connect with a student leader, such as a Resident Assistant, upon move in or as early in the semester as possible. Student leaders work with dynamic professional faculty and staff members to provide opportunities for new students to engage in conversations, programs, activities and social connections (Emmanuel College, 2018).

Partner with a Peer Mentor

Peer mentors are invaluable in initiating first-year students into the traditions and expectations on their campus. They help to highlight skills the new students already possess and point out skills that all students need to master in order to transition successfully (Carlile, 2016). In addition, peer mentors can share information and their experiences about stress management and academic burnout, time management, and connect them with campus resources for other specialized issues (Ahlquist, 2014). Mentors can refer students with serious concerns such as anxiety and depression to the health and counseling center on campus (Carlile, 2016). Mentors can also share their knowledge and experience about housing, meal plans, internships, classes and professors (Carlile, 2016).

Peer mentors are able to provide invaluable advice and guidance and offer an empathetic ear to first-year students as they remember and understand the nervousness associated with a new environment and new faces (Carlile, 2016). Furthermore, peer mentors are able to keep first-year students updated on important events, deadlines, and opportunities on campus (Carlile, 2016). Most importantly, mentors can model effective habits of academic success, such as participating in effective study groups and connecting with their professors (Ahlquist, 2014; Carlile, 2016).

College Readiness

Research has consistently shown that students who converse with faculty and peers, are challenged to perform at advanced levels, and receive frequent feedback have higher levels of academic performance and remain in college (Kuh, 2018). Although underserved student populations can benefit more from these activities, some students choose not to devote effort to them or other activities and as a result, leave college (Kuh,

2018). To increase the likelihood that students will stay in college and become engaged, educators must examine students' precollege experiences and the dispositions of those students who are less likely to engage and seek to induce them to participate in effective programs and practices (Kuh, 2018; Swail, Quinn, Landis, & Fung, 2012).

Success in college is strongly related to precollege academic preparation and achievement and not being grade-level proficient in reading and math at the eighth-grade benchmarks is a strong predictor of not being college ready at high school graduation (Kuh, 2018; Swail et al., 2012). Along with college-level academic skills, high school students must also develop study habits and other effective educational practices associated with success in college (Kuh, 2018).

Research demonstrates that more than 90% of high school seniors intend to go on to college but a good number of these students do not engage in the kinds of educational activities that will prepare them to succeed; for example, 47% of students reported that they only study for three or less hours per week, which is significantly below the 13-14 hours-per-week average of first-year students at four-year institutions (Kuh, 2018).

Student engagement declines from the first year of high school to the last year, and the overall engagement of seniors is much lower than any previous year (Kuh, 2018). In addition, data shows that first-year students expect to do more during their first 365 days of college than they actually do (Kuh, 2018). When asked, students reported that they actually studied two to six hours per week less than they thought they would when they started college (Kuh, 2018).

The gap between expectations and behavior can be found at the institutional level and extends beyond academics to cocurricular and extracurricular activities (Kuh, 2018). While a majority of first-year students expected to participate in activities, 32% of them were not involved in any sort of activity at all (Kuh, 2018). More than 75% of students expected their college to emphasize academics and attend campus events and interact with students from diverse backgrounds but found that their schools did not meet their expectations (Kuh, 2018).

Learning Communities

The structure of a college curriculum and the arrangement of resources can increase the chances a student will engage in productive activities; for example, providing students with frequent feedback is directly linked with college success (Kuh, 2018). Participation in first-year classes that have been created to build academic skills and foster social engagement has been shown to help students with academic challenges become more fully a part of college life with more frequent faculty interaction and more participation in the overall experience (Kuh, 2018).

One can define a learning community as an intentional program in which students are together in multiple courses so that they can form connections as they become initiated into college life (Villegas-Reimers, n.d.). As participants in learning communities, students work on projects together that are presented to the larger college community; through these activities, students get an opportunity naturally to be contributors to the community itself (Villegas-Reimer, n.d.).

If college students become connected to each other, this aids in their developing a strong sense of connection to their new environment, thus building a deep sense of belonging that has been shown to be connected to both persistence and overall student achievement (Villegas-Reimer, n.d.). Members of learning communities have measurably higher engagement in the wide gamut of campus activities, devote more hours to their academic studies, and have more relationships with different campus members (Kuh, 2018). The experiences that learning communities provide students allow them to gain more from college and can have positive effects, as demonstrated through student persistence through senior year (Kuh, 2018).

Benefits of learning communities. Learning communities organize students and faculty in smaller groups that encourage integration of the curriculum and help students establish academic and social support networks (Center for Engaged Learning, 2014; MDRC, 2012). Learning communities bring faculty together in more meaningful ways, focus students and faculty on learning outcomes, and provide a setting for community-based delivery of academic support programs (Center for Engaged Learning, 2014; Miller, 2018). In addition, these communities provide students with a setting to socialize and also to become acculturated to campus expectations and norms (Center for Engaged Learning, 2014).

Those who are part of a learning community tend to be higher academic performers, take part in best-practice activities, have better attendance, and are happier with their college experience (Center for Engaged Learning, 2014; MDRC 2012). Well-designed communities that emphasize collaborative learning show an improved result in student GPAs, higher college retention rates and satisfaction for undergraduate students, and fewer students on academic probation (Center for Engaged Learning, 2014; Miller, 2018).

Furthermore, students have reported an improvement in self-esteem, greater engagement in learning accompanied by an increased opportunity to write and speak, and intellectual empowerment (Center for Engaged Learning, 2014). Students also feel that participating in learning communities fosters a greater engagement in learning, provides them with a cohesive ability to meet academic and social needs, and exposes them to more complex thinking, a more complex world view, and a greater openness to ideas different than their own (Center for Engaged Learning, 2014). Connecting a student's academic experience to his or her social experience is a primary feature of learning communities and this connection can improve student involvement and feelings of connectedness within both social and academic realms (Center for Engaged Learning, 2014).

Best practices in creating learning communities. High-impact, educationally purposeful activities, such as learning communities, should be available for every student to participate in and institutions should ensure that at least two activities, one during the student's first year and one taken later in relation to his or her major, should be available (Center for Engaged Learning, 2014).

The Center for Engaged Learning (2014) defines a learning community as a small, connected group of learners that is influenced both by common goals and their relationships with one another. Effective learning communities are driven by student engagement, the willingness to invest their time, identity with the group, and the reciprocal influences of peers who are devoted to a common cause (Center for Engaged Learning, 2014; Miller, 2018). Student- centered learning is the priority and staff must realize that the individuals in the community are capable and can be entrusted with the responsibility for the quality and extent of their learning (Center for Engaged Learning, 2014).

Effective learning communities are the result of successful interaction and collaboration among faculty, students, and residence hall staff to intentionally achieve specific educational outcomes (Center for Engaged Learning, 2014; Miller, 2018). From the outset, learning communities should set out a specific and clear set of values and normative expectations for active participation as normative peer cultures of learning communities will enhance student learning and development (Center for Engaged Learning, 2014).

To achieve the best possible conditions for students, learning communities should have broad support from, and collaboration with, both faculty and staff. Stable leadership will ensure students have a greater chance of long-term stability and success (Center for Engaged Learning,

2014). The communities design and theme should be personally meaningful and relevant by appealing to not only students' academic goals, but their personal goals as well (Center for Engaged Learning, 2014).

Final Thoughts

Successful and effective transition programs assist new students entering college and can take many forms although the ultimate goal of any program is to instill students with the attitudes, knowledge, and skills that will enable them to be an engaged and productive member of their collegiate community.

Historically, summer bridge programs have been aimed toward underserved at-risk populations but are now common components of the preparation for all students as they begin their post-secondary studies. Other programs, such as student orientations, aim to make college processes, such as financial aid, simple and efficient while providing widespread support and resources across the board. No matter what transition program a student participates in, it is imperative that students and their families feel supported during the confusing and stressful transition to college.

Once at college, students who communicate with their faculty and peers, feel challenged in the classroom, and receive prompt and appropriate feedback, are more likely to persist. Those students that engage in a learning community are substantially more engaged, gain more from their college experience, and are the most likely to graduate and enter the professional world.

Points to Remember

- *Summer bridge programs have many benefits in supporting students' transitions to campus, both academically and socially.*
- *Transition programs can be the first chance a college has to engage new students into the culture, set forth the college's expectations, and educate the students on available resources. Peer mentors can be employed in these programs to introduce new students to the nuances of college life, share information and their experiences, and connect students with campus resources.*
- *Success in college is strongly related to precollege academic preparation and those students who participate in a*

transition program specifically designed to enhance their academic skills are more academically challenged, interact more with faculty, and express greater feelings of contentment with the quality of their college experience.
- *Learning communities can enhance a student's skills in both academic and social arenas while exposing students to more complex thinking, a more complex world view, and a greater openness to ideas different than their own.*

Chapter Four

Leadership for Learning: Leveraging Potential in all Students

To become a trustworthy student leader, an individual must first look inward and solidify his or her beliefs, ethics, standards, and values (Posner, 2018). These predetermined and closely held principles must guide every decision the student leader makes and, in this way, he or she communicates to the group what kind of a leader he or she is (Posner, 2018).

Student leadership is about motivating, influencing, and directing other people in an effort to work together and achieve the goals set forth by the team or organization (Ravisini, 2017). Through leadership, students will learn to build relationships, define identities, achieve tasks effectively, and display effective communication and interpersonal skills (Ravisini, 2017). Positive leaders have integrity and a strong character as well as myriad other qualities that should be developed as the leader grows, in turn encouraging "participation, honesty, and empathy in other individuals" (Allegheny College, 2018, n.p.).

Effective leaders should possess strong leadership characteristics and skills such as the ability to communicate, make decisions, organize and plan, think strategically, and manage risks (Nelson, 2017). Post-secondary institutions and future employers are looking for more modern skills such as resiliency, culture management, multi-generational management, collaboration, and emotional intelligence (Nelson, 2017). Those students with well-developed leadership skills will find themselves in a better place when it is time to job search.

Leadership Characteristics

There is a long, and widely undefined, list of personality traits that researchers believe enable an individual to help others succeed. According to Allegheny College (2018), necessary leadership skills include kindness, integrity, objectivity, initiative, forgiveness, and delegation. DuBrin (2016) includes self-confidence, humility, self-evaluation, trustworthiness, authenticity, extraversion, assertiveness, enthusiasm, optimism, warmth, and sense of humor on his list of leadership personality traits. Yet, each author or researcher has their own list of qualities that are thought to be the key to good leadership.

DuBrin (2016), takes the list one step further and includes "several task-related personality traits common to leaders" (p. 45) to include passion, flexibility and adaptability, courage, emotional intelligence, and an internal locus of control. Regardless of the skill or trait, DuBrin (2016), believes that those who strive to lead can begin to practice the "habits that lead to increased effectiveness" (p. 51).

Authenticity & Trustworthiness

Leaders that are consistent in what they say and do and remain true to their core values and personalities will gain the trust of others and will then lead others (Strang, 2013). Leaders, in order to be effective, "must learn to [clarify] their values and find the inner confidence necessary to express ideas, choose a direction, make tough decisions, act with determination, support others, and be able to take charge" (Posner, 2018, n.p.). Likewise, when students can align their attitudes, words, and motives with what actions they choose to take, they are more likely to be viewed by their peers as authentic and trustworthy (Strang, 2013).

Value Guided

Leaders have to make critical decisions that involve values, and these influence every aspect of life, such as moral judgments, communicating with others, and commitments to school and the community (Posner, 2018). Value systems create a set of limitations that guide the multitude of conscious and subconscious decisions and choices students must make every day (Posner, 2018). Having a clear set of values is essential for good leadership as the clearer students are about their values, the easier it is for them and their team to commit to the goals they have undertaken, particularly when faced with a difficult or challenging situation (Gleeson, 2017).

While clarifying their own values is essential, leaders must also possess the ability to be understanding of the values of those they lead and build alignment around those values (Posner, 2018). Research has shown that shared "values are the [mainstays] of productive and genuine working relationships [and successful leaders are able to] honor the uniqueness and individuality of all [group members while stressing] the common values of the group" (Posner, 2018, n.p.).

Extraversion & Enthusiasm

Most students in college leadership positions maintain an outgoing demeanor, show interest in other students, and gladly participate in group or team activities (Strang, 2013). To build rapport within a group and within the wider community, leaders must stay positive, be approachable, and express positive thoughts and feelings through verbal and nonverbal communication (Strang, 2013).

Emotional Intelligence, Flexibility & Adaptability

Student leaders should be able to empathize with others and recognize that their emotions, as well as group member emotions, can have an effect on the entire organization's performance (Strang, 2013). Groups and emotions are constantly in motion; therefore, good student leaders must be ready and willing to adjust to different settings and situations to bring about effective change. Great leaders will also have the willingness to take a risk on new ideas and not only put themselves in a position to be criticized or blamed, but also in a position where new ideas can successfully come to fruition (Strang, 2013).

When group members approach their leader "with questions or observations, positive leaders reward them by listening carefully to their words and [respond] in a way that demonstrates comprehension and empathy" (Allegheny College, 2018, n.p.). Leaders have the ability to ensure members feel heard and respected by listening to an explanation or reason why they "felt a certain way about an issue" (Allegheny College, 2018, n.p.).

Objectivity

Those leaders that have objectivity are able to give good feedback to their members and have the capability to distinguish a person's actions (Allegheny College, 2018). An objective leader will respond to a complicated situation is such a way that the critique is not personal, yet the behavior is addressed (Allegheny College, 2018).

Take Initiative

Student leaders who are action-oriented create change by proposing ideas or being supportive as others turn their own ideas into reality (Allegheny College, 2018). Successful leaders also see potential problem areas within their team and seek to address them immediately so that they do not get out of hand (Allegheny College, 2018).

Able to Delegate

Effective student leaders understand that they cannot perform all functions of the group on their own and take the initiative to involve other members in meaningful tasks (Wither, 2016). When leaders delegate tasks and responsibilities to other members in the group, those members will "feel needed and [that] they have invested their time wisely" (Allegheny College, 2018, n.p.).

Willingness

It is essential that a leader be able to work through differences when they occur within the group (Allegheny College, 2018). One of the key aspects of successful leadership is the ability to face conflicts with patience, compassion, and from a strong stance, including all members of the group to address any issues (Drumgoole, Jr., 2018). Conflict within a group and its subsequent resolution can have its benefits. When people within a group do not see eye to eye on an issue, leaders are presented with an opportunity to share stories, expand empathy, and create a greater awareness and understanding of each member's differences (Allegheny College, 2018).

Student Leadership Roles

The post-secondary campus has myriad clubs, organizations, and service learning opportunities that allow for all students to find something they feel confident enough to lead. With so many options, it is important to consider where the students' strengths are and how they can best be utilized.

Resident Adviser

Being a resident advisor of a dormitory enables students to build up their leadership skills by working with a team to mediate conflicts, build communities, help other students in need, and be a resource for their peers (Lucier, 2018b).

Campus Club/Organization

Students can make a difference on their campus whether they are in a significant and large leadership role, such as student body president, or a smaller role, such as a residence hall or cultural organization representative (Lucier, 2018b). Campus clubs often help the community with food drives and other such needs.

Student Newspaper

Although it may sound non-traditional, writing for the student newspaper has all the same principles of good leadership skills as other leadership roles on campus: time management, communication skills, taking a stance on a particular position, collaborating as part of a team, and working under pressure (Lucier, 2018b)

Civic Engagement and Community Service Projects

Civic engagement can promote avenues for student learning and global awareness to nurture the development of responsible, global citizens who are committed to building a sense of community and stand up for what is right and just in today's world (Georgia Tech, 2018). As leaders with civic engagement roles, for example, students can provide their peers with the opportunity to implement a major event, such as a fundraiser for a charity, and help them gain experience in planning and organizing, communication, and collaboration (Lucier, 2018b).

Athletics

Student athletes are called upon constantly to exhibit leadership skills, whether it be to motivate a teammate or help them to overcome adversity, give 110% at practice, or to maintain a positive attitude after losing a game (Life of an Athlete, 2018). The most influential leaders take ownership and responsibility for their mistakes and place personal success beneath the overall success of the team (Life of an Athlete, 2018).

On-Campus Employment

Working in on-campus employment, such as a work study job, allows student who do not want to be front and center as a leader to still gain experience about leadership by observing from a distance. Working with full-time employees in departments such as Residence Life or the Office of Student Engagement can help students see what leadership looks like behind the scenes and how to develop leaders in a formal, structured way (Lucier, 2018b).

Work in the Campus Admissions Office

Working with the campus admissions office offers students multiple opportunities, such as a tour guide or host, to lead new and prospective students and can help students demonstrate that they are responsible, respectful, and have the ability to communicate well with others (Lucier, 2018b).

Benefits of Being a Student Leader

Without question, being a student leader has immediate and long-term benefits. Short-term, individuals who seek leadership roles are able to help others and practice group organizational skills, while long-term, the student gets valuable experience that can be used when looking for a job. The benefits clearly outweigh the negatives and as students engage in team building, networking, problem solving, and more.

Team Building

One of the primary roles of being a student leader is the ability to build a team of people to collectively accomplish a goal (Scudamore, 2016). Beyond fundamental and modern leadership skills, student leaders have the unique ability to see the strengths and weaknesses of each of their team members and make the strengths of each individual member work for the whole entire team (Nelson, 217). Team building provides a platform to increase group collaboration, communicate clearly, build trust, and minimize conflicts (Scudamore, 2016).

Networking

Team building and student leadership during college enable students to build networks and connections at various levels; for example, student leaders get to know and work with faculty members, staff, administrators, leaders of student clubs and organizations, and local community members (Nelson, 2017). Strong leaders are able to introduce their team members to all these connections and even delegate a team member to be the primary contact in a networking relationship (Nelson, 2017). Once established at the college level, strong networking relationships can turn into highly valuable professional and personal contacts after college (Fredshaw, 2016).

Increased Responsibility

Students who undertake a leadership role while in college need to understand and accept that they have a newfound responsibility that can affect a wide range of people. They must make sure that their group members are fully participating and putting their best foot forward (Fredshaw, 2016). If one member fails to uphold their responsibilities or complete an assigned task, it becomes the leader's responsibility to hold them responsible while simultaneously finding a way to accomplish the goal (Zenger, 2015).

Increased Confidence

To succeed as a leader, students must first and foremost believe in themselves and their own abilities (Fredshaw, 2016). Whether it be participating in student government, starting and running a club, or organizing a fundraiser or other event, leading a campus organization is a great opportunity for students to develop the confidence they will need in the real world after graduation (Fredshaw, 2016). Leaders who are self-assured without being overbearing can instill self-confidence in their team members and assure them that they can overcome any challenges to reaching their ultimate goal (Strang, 2013).

Refined Problem-Solving Skills

Life can be one challenge after another, particularly at the college level when students are developing into young adults. Leaders are often given the task of guiding their team through endless challenges on top of an already demanding schedule of classes, personal obligations, and responsibility to effectively perform their leadership duties (Fredshaw, 2016). Achieving the balance between these responsibilities enables leaders to hone their problem-solving skills and enhance their ability to multi-task prior to entering the professional world beyond college (Griswold, 2013).

Becoming an Inspiration

Although students may find it difficult to be respected by their peers, those student leaders that do earn their peers' respect can become important role models for other students and adults across campus (Nelson, 2017). Becoming a role model for others also allows leaders the opportunity to build their confidence and communication skills by persuasively addressing their team members and other stakeholders on campus about the goals and purpose of their group (Fredshaw, 2016). Students will be able to build the poise and self-assuredness they will need later by serving as an inspiration to others through speaking at campus events, assisting incoming freshmen and transfer students, or working at other group events on campus (Fredshaw, 2016).

Effective Management

Leadership is not just about motivating but about the ability to manage a group of people, oversee operational procedures, formulate budgets, and devise what the priorities of the group should be. College is one of the few places that leaders are allowed to make mistakes and learn from them without dire consequences (Fredshaw, 2016).

Higher Capabilities

Students often arrive at college with preconceived ideas about what they can do and not do until they are suddenly forced to push their mental or physical boundaries (Fredshaw, 2016). By assuming a leadership role on campus, students will be in a position to step in and take care of specific tasks and responsibilities they have never been faced with before. For example, leaders may have to perform accounting functions or be in charge of creating ideas to promote their organization (Fredshaw, 2016). By taking on the challenge, students are able to discover new talents and realize they are capable of doing more than they thought, thus not only making them a stronger individual but a stronger leader as well.

Résumé Building

Leadership experience gained in college can be shown to a student's future potential employer and is more tangible than a grade point average alone (Fredshaw, 2016). Companies seeking to hire new graduates are looking for potential employees that have established leadership skills and can potentially advance to managerial positions (Fredshaw, 2016).

Ability to Negotiate

It is essential that student leaders are able to make those people involved in their group or organization feel respected and important (Fredshaw, 2016). By participating in frequent individual collaboration, leaders will gain the ability and skill to prioritize the different issues that can arise between group members and learn the art of compromise (Zohar, 2015). Negotiation skills may also be enhanced through participation in any college-run workshops or leadership development opportunities on cooperative learning and conflict resolution (Fredshaw, 2016).

Final Thoughts

Student leaders bring to their team a set of deeply held beliefs, values, standards, ethics, and ideals that they draw on to make genuine decisions and pursue actions for the benefit of the group. These core values and principles are also used to motivate, influence, and direct team members in a collaborative effort to achieve the group's stated goals and ambitions.

As leaders, college students are able to build relationships, become more aware of their self-identity, and develop their interpersonal skills. Qualities such as strength of character and integrity can be developed through participation in the group, honesty among members, and maintaining empathy and understanding for each and every student.

The development of strong leadership skills, such as communication, decision-making, strategic thinking, culture management, and emotional intelligence are becoming more important and students that possess these skills are highly sought after by potential employers. Leaders that are emotionally intelligent and have the capability to understand the values of others are able to build alignment within their group, creating genuine working relationships that value and embody the individuality and differences among all group members.

Being a leader in college comes with newfound responsibility and obligations beyond academics, work, and family. Effective leaders are able to motivate and ensure that all group members participate to the extent that they can and put their best food forward in an effort towards success. Leaders must keep in mind that for those students who become unreliable and unable to hold up their responsibilities and obligations, they must not only address the issue, but take on the responsibility for accomplishing that member's goal.

Student life presents multiple challenges and leaders have the responsibility of guiding their team members through these challenges while helping them find a way to achieve a balance between all their academic and outside obligations, all on top of balancing their own life. Some leaders will be faced with responsibilities and called upon to perform new tasks. By pushing their own boundaries, leaders can rise to new heights by doing what they once thought was not possible, making them not only a strong leader, but a stronger individual who has much to offer in the world after college.

Points to Remember

- *Authentic leaders keep their word and follow through. Holding true to their core values and finding the necessary confidence to express unique ideas and make tough decisions will gain leaders the much sought after respect and trust of their peers.*

- *Organizations and their members are made up of a diverse array of students and effective leaders are able to recognize individual's emotions and are willing to adjust their actions to different situations so effective change can happen.*
- *The willingness of a leader to take a risk and be criticized when that risk fails makes them more authentic and group members more likely to support new ideas and allow those ideas and risks to come to a successful realization.*
- *Student leadership and team building while in college allows students to establish connections at multiple levels that will serve as a professional network of valuable personal and professional contacts after college.*

Chapter Five

Connections Outside of the Classroom: Building College-Community Partnerships

In today's world, there is a decline in civic participation among college-aged students and our society as a whole (New, 2016). Institutes of higher education have begun to recognize this decline and have been making a conscious effort to return to their historic mission and foundational purpose of preparing graduates for a life of involved and committed citizenship (Fong, 2014; Kniffin & Clayton, 2017). Participation in civic engagement will prepare students for a life of purpose and instill an ethos of working for the common good (Fong, 2014). As such, colleges and universities are now doing more than training students for a profession. New forms of civic engagement are not only preparing students to be good citizens, but also ensuring that students leave with the understanding that they can use the knowledge and skills gained with education for their career and for the public good (New, 2016; Fong, 2014).

Research has demonstrated that students want to participate in actions that will repair and resolve the problems they see in the world. Nearly 40% of students feel that becoming a community leader is a very important and/or an essential life goal, while almost 60% of first year students report that there is a very good chance they will vote in a local, state or national election while in college (New, 2016).

Participating in civic engagement and service learning provides a platform for students to use what they have learned in the classroom to create solutions to real-world issues (New, 2016). Research has also shown that employers regard evidence of social responsibility as a desirable trait in potential hires (Fong, 2014).

Partnerships between higher education and local community organizations, particularly nonprofit and mission-driven organizations, will not only provide a community with enthusiastic volunteers, the students will gain authentic educational experiences that can affect their community in a positive way (Loria, 2018). These partnerships can foster the belief that student success is a mutual responsibility, help uncover obstacles that can hinder student success, and generate collaborative solutions (Public Agenda, 2017). Through these partnerships, community partners will also gain a new understanding of the college's work toward student success and college faculty will be able to take advantage of new professional development opportunities (Public Agenda, 2017).

Creating College-Community Partnerships

Every community has authentic needs that must be addressed and met, yet it is first essential that community members become involved (Bridgman et al., 2018). College provides a unique opportunity for students to become involved in a unified goal and cross barriers that may divide student and academic affairs (Bridgman et al., 2018; Fuchs, Cannella, Pisano, 2014).

There is a growing concern among higher education that there is an absence of community awareness and that a single, self-focused, ego-centered perspective has begun to dominate our college culture (Bridgman et al., 2018). Civic engagement can help students develop a selfless perspective as well as enhance their understanding of something other than themselves and their immediate environment, thus serving as a vehicle for positive social change (Fuchs et al., 2014).

Through civic engagement, the outside community has the opportunity to be a co-educator and to benefit from any contributions the students can make, such as creativity, problem solving, and their desire to make a difference (Bridgman et al., 2018). Students become engaged citizens when they can partake in a variety of activities that build skills and cognate knowledge and offer them opportunities to act as positive leaders and change agents. When this occurs, students are instilled with a sense of civic awareness and civic responsibility (Bridgman et al., 2018; Fuchs et al., 2014).

When deciding on partnership opportunities, instructors may wish to build credibility with an organization by starting with a small project defined in scope so that students can demonstrate responsible and effective civic engagement (Loria, 2018). Once a solid and trusting relationship has been established, students will be more likely to invest in these projects from conception to construction, where the timeframe is longer, often lasting a semester or academic year (Loria, 2018).

After community agents have agreed to work with an institution, instructors should hold discussions with both the students and the community representative. The focus of such talks is on the value of the work to be undertaken, both in terms of its relationship to the college's missions and values and in what it contributes to the community. Demonstrating relevancy and meaningfulness will show the practical applicability of the class lesson and keep the students engaged in their role within the partnership (Loria, 2018). Students can also view their work commitment contextually—both as something that benefits the community and that is part of a larger fabric (Loria, 2018).

To create strong, long-term, successful partnerships, community partners must provide students with the opportunity to become more active in participation in the broader community; this requires that they acquire skills that round out their more traditional education. At the same time, students must demonstrate how their work within the community will further the organization's mission (Loria, 2018). This shared vision will allow both partners to work toward mutual success (Fuchs et al., 2014).

Effective communication and collaboration is essential between both partners and it should be agreed upon at the beginning of the relationship who will own the relationship and who will communicate progress and challenges to improve the experience (Loria, 2018). Depending on the partnership, students may even be able to take a leadership role to gain valuable experience (Loria, 2018). Community partners not only serve as leaders, they serve as educators and should be empowered to think of themselves in that role with students (Loria, 2018).

Partnerships with Community Colleges

Community colleges are the nation's gateway to gainful employment, yet the current generation of college-age students will be less educated than their parents' generation and will be unable to compete in a national landscape that is increasingly demanding high-level job skills (Public Agenda, 2017). Community colleges can ensure a rigorous and relevant academic experience for students through creative partnerships with the community that provide a clear, coherent, and high-quality educational experience that is not only challenging and engaging, but also gives students the experience they need to meet their educational and career goals (Mangan, 2018; Shields & Singleton, 2014). Community colleges must ensure that their students' educational paths lead to career advancement and/or further education and to do this, they should focus on partnerships with transfer institutions and potential employers to create clear, rigorous, and relevant programs of study (Public Agenda, 2017).

Partnerships between faculty members at the community college level and faculty at four- year institutions should aim to provide community college students with more project-based experiences and undergraduate research opportunities to ensure the community college curricula and programs of study are clearly aligned with labor market needs and the program requirements of the four-year institutions (Shields & Singleton, 2014; Public Agenda, 2017). Likewise, community colleges can partner with employers in high-growth sectors to provide work experience programs for students, such as internships, co-ops and job shadowing (Xu, Ran, Fink, Jenkins, & Dundar, 2018).

Strategies to Engage the Community Within Higher Education

Various strategies including focus groups, dialogue sessions, and community forums can be employed to reach out to community stakeholders to raise awareness, gain insight, and build the common ground needed for effective collaboration (Shields & Singleton, 2014). Focus groups allow for the exploration of issues and give colleges an opportunity to understand stakeholder attitudes and interests, frame any issues to be discussed, develop background materials for deeper engagement, and identify issues that could threaten collaboration (Public Agenda, 2017).

While focus groups can achieve some community engagement goals, illuminate confusion, and clarify differences in priorities, they do not help communities effectively communicate and collaborate to build the common ground needed to best serve students (Public Agenda, 2017). As focus groups are also research based, colleges may want to engage in stakeholder dialogues as well. Participants in these dialogues are stakeholders external to the college community, such as local employers or staff from community-based organizations, which voluntarily contribute their time and ideas (Xu et al., 2018).

Stakeholder dialogues allow for productive discussions regarding the work of the college that elicits the community's interest and ideas and identifies opportunities for collaboration (Public Agenda, 2017; Shields & Singleton, 2014). As these conversations are less structured than focus groups, they are more likely to serve as a vehicle for relationship-building and for the cultivation of relational trust between colleges and potential community partners (Public Agenda, 2017).

In addition to focus groups and stakeholder dialogues, community forums can be used to engage a broad cross-section of a community in dialogue about the work of a college (Xu et al., 2018). Conversations with the whole community reach the largest number of people, gain the broadest input, and provide fresh insight for the college, external stakeholders and all community members equally. College practitioners may begin to understand their work in new ways, formal stakeholders in the community will be able to connect their priorities to those of the college, and the insights and experiences of students and families become vital resources for problem solving and creative collaboration (Public Agenda, 2017).

Strategies to Engage the Student Within the Community

There are several approaches that institutions of higher education can take to get students engaged in the community. One approach is to create a civic engagement requirement using either first year seminars for all students or specific programs with sequential course requirements over the course of multiple years (Project Pericles, Inc., 2018). Another option is the pathways approach, which pulls together a list of courses, co-curricular opportunities, and service projects organized around specific themes such as education/access, food/sustainability, health, or specific learning outcomes (Project Pericles, Inc., 2018).

Civic scholars' programs are specialized, and distinct programs created for a cohort of civic engagement scholars offer three or four year experiences in which students take a series of courses and seminars and participate in structured community-based learning or service projects (Project Pericles, Inc., 2018). Other programs, such as a certificate program, can also be offered that will attract students to civic engagement opportunities and recognize any work the students may already be doing (Project Pericles, Inc., 2018).

Institutions might also wish to proceed with an open choice model of civic engagement. These approaches can vary widely from campus to campus and can include independent civic engagement courses created by faculty members working independently from their colleagues and are not associated with a campus-wide civic engagement program (Project Pericles, Inc., 2018). For other faculty, their efforts to create civic engagement courses are part of a concerted strategy to encourage and develop civic engagement opportunities on campus and are supported by a very active civic engagement center (Project Pericles, Inc., 2018).

Discussion Boards

Discussion boards, particularly as part of a course on civic engagement, are not only an effective tool in the academic environment, but also a way to nurture a sense of community among students (Bridgman et al., 2018). Research has shown that when controversial, thought-provoking questions are posted for class discussion, students have the highest quality participation, including student feedback and spin-off discussions (Bridgman, et al., 2018). Often, students that are too shy to speak in class are provided with an effective outlet to have an equal voice and right to speak (Bridgman et al., 2018).

Social bonds that are built through discussion boards can provide a sense of group connectedness and important socio-affective and cognitive benefits; these may include advanced modes of higher order thinking, as well as advanced reading and writing skills (Bridgman et al., 2018). Discussions also enhance students' abilities to examine specific situations and to effect desired changes and voice ideas and opinions articulately in public (Bridgman et al., 2018). Discussion boards are valuable in that they encourage students in offering up their own experiences and those of their peers to build and cultivate knowledge as well as use their voice in inclusive, diverse, problem-solving conversations that are directly connected to action and change (Bridgman et al., 2018).

Service-Learning Courses

Service-learning brings together the knowledge, questions, resources, and priorities of the community with those of educational institutions to advance public purposes (Clayton & Kniffin, 2017). Service-learning partnerships are purposefully designed around a student's specific learning goals so that academic content can be integrated with relevant experience. It is this synergistic integration of academic material, relevant service activities, and critical reflection that allows students, faculty, and community members to engage and achieve academic, civic, and personal learning objectives and advance public purposes (Clayton & Kniffin, 2017).

Critical reflection is central to engaged learning in that it makes meaning of a student's experience and can generate deep learning and improve the quality of action (Clayton & Kniffin, 2017). Individuals' concepts of and commitment to a more just and equitable world can be influenced by academic activities that involve civic learning in a variety of forms (Clayton & Kniffin, 2017). This orientation toward change and capacity building can generate short/long-term improvements in individual and community well-being and the systems within which they live (Clayton & Kniffin, 2017).

Students benefit from service-learning courses "academically, professionally, and personally" (University of Minnesota, 2018, n.p.). Academically, students can better grasp course materials and develop the higher-order critical thinking and problem-solving skills; in turn, these skills give them the ability to deal with nuanced learning as they become more receptive to change and cognitively more flexible (University of Minnesota, 2018).

Professionally, students can gain hands-on experience and develop or enhance a cluster of necessary skills, such as the ability to communicate effectively, collaborate with others, and exert leadership (University of Minnesota, 2018). Service-learning projects in the community permit an early chance to evaluate one's skills, interests, and values in a potential career path or learn more about a field that interests them. Students gain connections to professionals and community members, forming valuable mentorship and networking relationships that later might lead to potential employment and internships (University of Minnesota, 2018).

Personally, students will be able to explore, and even cement, a system of values. Through various opportunities, students will be able to act upon those beliefs and values, gain knowledge and a new understanding of the diverse cultures and communities around them, and learn more about social issues and their root causes (University of Minnesota, 2018).

Higher education faculty can also benefit personally and professionally from integrating service-learning into their courses. Teaching with service-learning will encourage interactive teaching methods and reciprocal learning between students and faculty, which could then lead to new avenues for research and publication (University of Minnesota, 2018). By engaging in active learning, instructors will be able to involve students with different learning styles and add new insights and dimensions to class discussions, potentially boosting course enrollment by attracting highly motivated and engaged students (University of Minnesota, 2018).

To embed the culture of service into the college curriculum, faculty are not only designing community-based service learning courses, they are serving as mentors for civic engagement student leaders (Fong, 2014). As mentors, instructors are able to further develop students' civic and leadership skills, foster relationships between faculty and the community organizations, and provide firsthand knowledge of community issues and opportunities for students to be more involved in those issues (University of Minnesota, 2018).

Community partners also benefit from service-learning courses and projects as they will gain the additional human resources that may be needed to achieve their organizational goals (University of Minnesota, 2018). Organizations will better be able to reach out to youth to not only educate them about community issues and increase the public's awareness of key issues but, more importantly, correct any misconceptions they may have (University of Minnesota, 2018).

Final Thoughts

With the decline in civic participation among college-aged students, institutes of higher education are now, more than ever, preparing their graduates for a life of involved and committed citizenship through participation in civic engagement opportunities that will prepare them for a life of purpose. Students should be assured that when they leave college they will have the knowledge and skills they need for their career and to serve the public in a positive and meaningful way.

Strong partnerships between colleges and their surrounding community will forge a sense of shared responsibility for student success and lead to collaborative solutions that will assist students in overcoming any obstacles they may face in pursuit of not only academic success, but life success. In addition, partnerships will provide the meaningfulness, relevancy, and practical applicability of their coursework that students crave. When students can place their academic work into a real life context, they will become more invested and engaged in their education and know that their efforts are part of a larger, more meaningful world context.

To provide students with civic engagement opportunities that are meaningful and relevant, colleges can create civic engagement requirements, such as first year seminars, specific programs, such as the civic scholars program, co-curricular opportunities, and service-learning projects. Opportunities such as service-learning are beneficial in that they integrate academic content with relevant experience and bring together the knowledge, questions, resources, and priorities of the community with those of the institution. This synergistic integration of academic material, relevant service activities, and critical reflection will allow colleges and their students to engage and achieve academic, civic, and personal learning objectives and successes, all while advancing the good of the surrounding community.

Points to Remember

- *Civic engagement and, more specifically, service learning, allows students to use what they have learned in the classroom to create solutions to real-world issues and allows communities to serve as co-educators.*
- *Strong, long-term, successful partnerships between colleges and the community are created when students have the opportunity to become more involved, engaged members of the community and acquire skills complementary to their education.*
- *Community colleges are in a unique position to ensure students have a clear, coherent, relevant, and meaningful academic experience through community partnerships that give students the experience they need to meet their educational and career goals.*
- *Community forums not only engage an entire community in dialogue about the work of a college, they also provide a mechanism for the broadest input and fresh insight for the college. Through these forums, colleges and formal stakeholders can connect their priorities, allowing students, families, and other community members to become vital resources in problem solving and creative collaboration.*

Chapter Six

Advancing Academic Advising: Assets-Based Approaches to Student Development

One of the most critical elements of a successful college experience is a meaningful and supportive relationship between student and advisor. When considering both a student's academic success and emotional well-being, it is difficult to imagine anyone more crucial in the creation of a positive higher education experience, from start to finish. In many institutions, however, advising is seen as an ancillary role, taking a back seat to teaching, research, and athletics. On campuses that captivate, engage, and retain their students, advising is elevated to an instrumental developmental role and attention is paid to all aspects of the advising relationship.

Advising in college has been conceptualized in different ways over time. One major shift in concepts is represented by the evolution of the role of advisor/mentor from traditional notions of purely academic advising to contemporary approaches that are more rooted in the field of counseling psychology, as well. Tinto (1993), Bean (2005), and Kuh et al. (2005b) see advising as integrally linked to college retention to graduation, with the advisor able to play a powerful role in encouraging and guiding the advisee in ways that help him or her recognize strengths, overcome challenges, and reach full potential.

Due to increasing diversity on college campuses today, there is a greater need for a broader concept of the advisor role (Huber & Miller, 2013). Advisors can only do this effectively in settings that support professional development, reward effective advisors for their work, provide dedicated time for meaningful counseling, make available necessary resources to support extracurricular advising activities, and make thoughtful matches of the dyads (Huber & Miller, 2013).

The History of College Advising

Miars (2017) provided a quick snapshot of the history of academic advising in this country that moved from formal relationships to the more recent concept of developmental advising. Miars (2017) describes the eras this way:

- The first era (1620 to 1870): Academic advising goes unrecognized: It took a while for the idea of advising to catch on. Prior to the American Revolution, relationships between students and professors were strictly formal and hierarchical. Students would only have direct contact with faculty for disciplinary reasons. The first advisors emerged in the mid-1800s, though they were more akin to tutors and often recent graduates.
- The second era (1870 to 1970): Academic advising remains unexamined: Across this second era, more institutions established advising roles, usually filled by faculty, in response to curricular expansion and the emergence of undergraduate majors. As early as 1889, many felt that advisors were spending too much time on course and major selection and not enough time building relationships—a complaint that has persisted for 130 years. With the dawn of retention theory in the 1960s and 1970s, new structures for advising emerged, driven by a holistic focus on the student. Other challenges arose that still affect advising today—faculty disengagement and fear of coddling among them—and there was vast inconsistency across advising programs.
- The third era (1970 to 2003): Academic advising is (slowly) examined: Enrollment in higher education increased dramatically during the 1960s to 1980s, as did attrition, which led to the continued expansion of academic advising. Familiar terms like "professional advising," "developmental advising," and "advising as teaching" cropped up during a new phase of scholarship that included the formation of NACADA in 1979. The rise of dedicated advisors meant more visibility and assessment, though the profession continued to be largely undervalued and underfunded (Miars, 2017).

Cook (2001, 2009) finds parallels in the trajectory of both academic advising as a field and the history of higher education itself, with particular emphasis on the nature of student personnel work. With very few (male) students attending the first American colleges and universities, it was not difficult for the college president and its faculty to be student advisors; "advising," in the country's early history, meant attending to the young men's academic and moral needs.

Faculty roles, however, were soon to change, with the Morrill Acts of 1863 and 1869; these prompted the founding of land-grant colleges as well as Black colleges and universities, diversifying both the curriculum and the student population (National Research Council, 1995). As coeducation was born, it became the catalyst for "deans of women," perhaps the forerunner of advisors to come. Kenyon College (OH) established the first formal advising system in 1841, and there were many variations of this system in decades to come; for example, in 1906, Columbia began its advising system to supervise the selection of classes and narrow the widening gap between faculty and students (Cook, 2001; 2009).

In 1911, Reed College offered the first credit-bearing orientation course and Brown University followed with orientation lectures to orient students to the goals of a college education (Cook, 2001, 2009). The emphasis on the importance of a successful freshman year became salient among institutions as did the emphasis on counseling students. As early as 1932, the University of Chicago established fundamental principles for counseling its students (Cook, 2009). Among these principles were concern for the whole person; recognition of the difficulty of transitioning to college; the relationship between academic and nonacademic affairs; the necessity of relational learning, developed over time by continuous relationships with an advisor; the suitability of individuals for the counseling role; and the preference for one's academic advisor to provide counseling (Cook, 2009).

Post-World War II saw a large influx of veterans move on to college campuses, and they required greater attention to student personnel work (Young, Michael, & Jean, 2018). This elevated student affairs work, yet faculty members were still seen as primary advisors until the 1960s, when advising was differentiated from counseling and peer and professional advising models were initiated.

In the 1970s with an increasing number of diverse students entering higher education institutions, the growth of community colleges, open enrollment and federal programs to support those with disabilities, from lower income brackets, and first-generation students, colleges were forced to expand and specialize their academic advising and rethink the definition of advising itself (Cook, 2009).

Historically, there had been a separation and division of labor when working with students on a college campus. The class differentiations in definitions are provided by Grites (2013)

> *(a) faculty advising, and activity dispatched by members of the teaching faculty and directed towards assisting students in their educational, vocational, and personal concerns at a defined level of competence, and (b) counseling, which enlists the efforts of persons who are specifically trained and experienced in the areas of educational, psychological, or clinical counseling procedures* (p. 46).

Only in the early 1980s did colleges begin to marry these two functions into what became termed developmental advising (Grites, 2013).

Developmental advising required that advisors consider more than academics and delve into their advisees' goals, dreams, personal attributes, and hopes for the future. This more wholistic model expanded each advisor's role and asked him or her to help advisees in the realms of career, education, and personal growth and development (Grites, 2013). While some faculty flourished in this growing role, others saw this as an intrusion on their time and efforts in the academic sphere that they felt that had been recruited to operate in.

The most influential proponent of developmental advising was Chickering (1969), whose work codified the developmental tasks of young adulthood and their relation to college success. Chickering (1969) described the developmental tasks as gaining a sense of competence, learning to manage emotions, developing autonomy, establishing a unique identity, developing more mature and diverse relationships, developing a sense of personal purpose, and arriving at integrity through forming authentic core values and beliefs. In order to assist their advisees in mastering these tasks, Chickering (1969) urged advisors to envision themselves as wearing three hats informational, relational, and skilled. This required that they be able to form meaningful relationships with their students, impart necessary knowledge, and build advisees' conceptual abilities (Chickering, 1969). Now, beyond the traditional academic advising, faculty needed to become skilled in helping their students become goal setters, problem solvers, and co-creators of their future plans.

Developmental advising requires that the advisor be able to accurately assess the developmental stages and needs of students so that the advisors can develop interventions to help students move to higher levels of cognitive, emotional, social, and career development (Grites, 2013).

Students enter college at a wide variety of developmental levels, and their levels may vary intra-individually; for example, a student may be extremely advanced cognitively but lag in the social domain. Having a good command of questions that may help both advisor and advisee ascertain developmental stages and growth needs is key to this approach (Damminger & Rakes, 2017).

With the shift in definitions and the expansion of advisor roles, the field of academic advising now became more advisee-centered, at the same time that teaching became more learner-centered. Grites (1979) defined this new sense of an advising "decision-making process in which students realize their maximum educational potential through communication and information exchanges with an advisor" (p. 1). Developmental academic advising was defined as

> *a) a process; b) concerned with human growth; c) goal related; d) based on the establishment of a caring human relationship; e) offered by adult role models and mentors; f) the cornerstone of collaboration between student affairs and academic affairs; and g) inclusive of all campus and community resources* (Winston, Enders, & Miller, 1982, p. 7).

Creamer & Creamer (1994) wrote one of the earliest articles on actually translating developmental advising theory into practice. These authors defined goal categories for student growth as (1) setting career and life goals, (2) building self-insight and esteem, (3) broadening interests, (4) establishing meaningful interpersonal relationships, (5) clarifying personal values and styles of life, and (6) enhancing critical thinking skills and reasoning. Creamer & Creamer (1994) point out that even simple, pragmatic advisee questions such as "how can I avoid academic suspension?" or "how can I change majors?" are intertwined with personal development concerns and are ripe for advisor teaching. A prescriptive advisor might miss these subtle opportunities, but the savvy advisor will see these as opportunities for a student's growth in many domains.

There are myriad activities that Creamer & Creamer (1994) suggest for either individual or group advising. These developmental activities range from values clarification exercises, career exploration, and journal reflective writing to critical incident writing, personal dilemma resolution exercises, and goal-setting work (Creamer & Creamer, 1994). It is also suggested that group activities such as sessions on academic achievement, guided participation in campus events, discussions about campus climate issues, and multicultural encounter-like groups be included in group advising (Creamer & Creamer, 1994).

Such strategies suggest that the best possible advising is nested in a series of campus-supported activities. Captivating campuses recognize that advising is the responsibility of all personnel and offices. In the era of limited resources, it also makes sense to bundle activities where possible.

Establishing Core Competencies

In 2017, the National Academic Advising Association, or NACADA, decided that it needed to establish an articulated model of the advising core competencies. They describe the three-part model as follows:

- The "conceptual component provides the context for the delivery of academic advising" (NACADA, 2017, n.p.). It covers the ideas and theories that advisors must understand to effectively advise their students.
- The Informational component provides the substance of academic advising. It covers the knowledge advisors must gain to be able to guide the students at their institution.
- The Relational component provides the skills that enable academic advisors to convey the concepts and information from the other two components to their advisees.

According to NACADA (2017), an effective advisor must understand these components and their interactions.

At the conceptual level, a competent advisor knows the history and role expectations, theories undergirding sound practice, different approaches and techniques to use with different advisees, the desired outcomes of a sound relationship between advisor and advisee, and the means by which inclusive environments are created and sustained (NACADA, 2017).

Informational concerns are broad in scope but encompass the information needed to impart accurate information to advisees (NACADA, 2017). These include all information about the institution's academic offerings, requirements, policies and regulations. The aforementioned are the items that traditionally have defined academic advising in its narrowest form.

Today, academic advisors also need to understand the legal aspects of advising, including the need to protect an advisee's privacy and confidentiality (NACADA, 2017). They also need a broad awareness of the background characteristics and implied assets and needs of a hugely diverse student population; while being equally cognizant of college and community resources that different student constituencies might need so that they can make meaningful referrals when necessary (NACADA, 2017).

Most contemporary advisors also are tech-savvy and may employ technological means to stay in touch with their advisees.

The relational component of NACADA's (2017) model involves many techniques derived from counseling theory. This begins with creating rapport and building a relationship of genuine regard and trust. Communications from advisor to advisee need to be inclusive and respectful. A great deal of an advisor's work involves planning and conducting individualized sessions that meet each student's needs. In such sessions, advisors help students understand their academic experience, learn how to solve problems and overcome challenges, set personal goals, and make meaning out of their time on campus. Good advisors also find ways to assess their practice and refine it based upon feedback and insights (NACADA, 2017).

Burke, Sauerheber, Hughey, and Laves (2017) stress some other important counseling techniques that should be interwoven into good advising. These begin with an acceptance of the student as an individual and using that as a starting point for all interactions. Advisors must see their role as thinking and brainstorming, problem-solving and decision-making with the advisee, not for him or her (Burke et al., 2017). Good advisors and counselors do not assume that they understand a student's world view but strive to get him or her to articulate it for the counselor. Proper boundaries should be maintained, but a genuine alliance must be formed if trust and rapport are to be established.

Theories of Academic Advising

Over time, theories of academic advising have emerged, although not a great deal of research on the efficacy of such theories has been conducted. As theories evolved, they have become more developmental in nature and borrowed liberally from the counseling field and knowledge of lifespan psychology. With increasingly diverse college populations, changes to our theories of best practice in academic advising have likewise changed. Schreiner (2013) provided a brief history of the predominant paradigms in higher education.

Using Student Strengths as the Basis for Advising

Also called strengths-based advising, assets-based advising grew out of burgeoning research and applications of positive psychology and resiliency, and aspects of each were integrated into advising models (Schreiner, 2013). In the 1960s and '70s, the ranks of college-goers swelled, as institutions actively recruited a more diverse population; this required a paradigm shift to models of deficit remediation, as the gap in preparation for post-secondary success between traditional populations and those from lower-SES and first-generation families, who had generally attended high schools that provided a less-competitive education, was recognized (Schreiner, 2013).

Schreiner (2013) notes that contemporary counselors focus more and more on what is called either assets-based or strengths-based advising. This change has derived from growing recognition that every student brings with him or her coping mechanisms and personal and cultural assets that have served the student well in reaching college. Assets-based approaches leave behind the urge to begin with what is wrong or lacking in a student's academic background and focus instead on utilizing existing talents to overcome possible challenges once in college (Schreiner, 2013).

The model unfolds in a five-step process. First, advisors help students identify their talents; this can be done verbally or with other exercises such as writing (Schreiner, 2013). Once this step is accomplished, the savvy advisor helps each advisee see how what s/he already possesses can be translated into campus-based strengths (Schreiner, 2013). These strengths might be used in the classroom, in social situations, or in special venues such as sports, clubs or leadership roles. Third, advisors have students dream and articulate their desired futures; envisioning these futures, according to Schreiner (2013), provides motivation and energy - critical to surviving the inevitable challenges that students will face. The fourth step helps advisees break down the larger dream goals into manageable, smaller steps (Schreiner, 2013). Finally, advisors teach transferability of assets, allowing advisees to envision how they might use an asset in one arena in another one, such as using strategies that work in athletics to help them in the classroom (Schreiner, 2013).

Damminger & Rakes (2017) note that unlike developmental advising, which uses open ended questions, assets-based advising is designed to immediately help students reflect on their abilities to succeed. To create this awareness that they are competent individuals who have used effective strategies when faced with hurdles in the past, advisors might use a script that includes questions such as:

- What are your biggest assets?
- What are some of your proudest accomplishments?
- Which subjects do you enjoy the most and come easiest to you?
(Damminger & Rakes, 2017).

Advising to Promote Self-Authorship

Kegan (1994) and Baxter Magolda (2008) are credited with the emergence of self-authorship theory. In this theory, an advisor centers on helping his or her advisees grow as unique individuals and emerging adults. This entails the delicate process of examining the beliefs and values inherited from one's family of origin, culture and community and eventually arriving at those that are more aligned with one's authentic self.

The advisor supports his advisees as they learn to examine and question the goodness of fit of external requirements such as parental expectations, faculty expectations, cultural models of success, as well as the student's own internal desires and intentions (Kegan, 1994). This often is an extremely painful journey due to the possibility that the individual's past may clash with what the student is experiencing in his or her new environment.

Baxter Magolda (2008) described this as a time when internal voices and external values clash –a crossroads of sorts. Drake, Jordan, & Miller (2013) mention, however, that many students choose to leave the dissonance of the crossroads unresolved because it is too painful to make change, or they may not even recognize the dissonance.

Johnson (2017) believes that advising from a self-authorship stance is crucial to first-year college success as:

> *First-year students may seek out academic advisors during the academic planning process to gain approval for their ideas. The plans they articulate may represent a conglomeration of predetermined career paths, parental expectations, and knowledge of subjects they feel they have mastered and for which they feel confident* (p. 155).

Advisors are tasked with gently moving "students towards self-authorship by co-constructing these plans with them" (Johnson, 2017, p. 155). Nudging involves posing questions that require reflection and help students get in touch with their own voices while decision-making.

When students reach a crossroads, the skilled advisor/mentor can play a hugely transformative role. S/he can validate the advisee as a knower, lend support as the student arrives at a more self-authored path, and also acknowledge how hard it may be to travel that path (Johnson, 2017). Many times, students encounter resistance from the home front, so the advising sessions may provide a safe space for using reflective conversations to decompress from that resistance, learn strategies to navigate this new terrain, and align emerging values and goals with actions (Johnson, 2017).

Advising as Teaching

This approach is based on a learner-centered philosophy that recognizes the similarities between the two activities (Damminger & Rakes, 2017). This begins with the recognition that quality teachers and advisors establish positive relationships with students, set goals, and share the responsibility for the outcomes (Reynolds, 2010). The same attributes that make for a good classroom experience are used in the advising relationship to include active learning, problem-solving, high expectations, assessment and feedback, personal relevance, making connections that facilitate personal and academic growth, and a career focus (Damminger & Rakes, 2017).

Reynolds (2010) presents six principles for incorporating learning principles into advising practices. These begin with recognition that active learning is far more effective than passive learning. This means that advisees must have an equal role in everything from articulating their goals and identifying their strengths to breaking goals down into manageable steps, knowing how to assess if they are on target, having strategies for dealing with getting off track, and recognizing goal attainment (Reynolds, 2010). These steps comprise the second principle, which is that learning is more effective and efficient with well-articulated, reasonable, and meaningful goals (Reynolds, 2010).

High expectations for learners and advisees are critical in promoting growth and achievement (Reynolds, 2010). This principle often can cause initial concern or anxiety among students who doubt their ability to master a task; they may appear unmotivated, but the skilled advisor or faculty member can apply the fourth principle, which is an understanding that motivation is malleable (Reynolds, 2010). Students can become energized to push beyond their perceived capabilities if they feel supported by their advisors and can understand the lofty task as a series of doable steps.

Reynolds (2010) also points out that all college students require feedback early and frequently. Yet eventually, over time, students must develop the internal capacity for accurate reflection and self-assessment. Learning to give oneself feedback is one of the hardest tasks of transitioning to college. Finally, advisees need positive interaction with their advisors; but it is also valuable if the advisor can find ways to promote interaction among advisees as well (Reynolds, 2010). It can be particularly meaningful to have more veteran advisees' mentor newer ones, providing perspectives that can only come from student-to-student conversations.

In a study by Delaney, Edwards, Jensen, and Skinner (2010), there was an identifiable set of nine characteristics that research participants linked to effective teaching to include a faculty member who was respectful, knowledgeable, approachable, engaging, organized, responsive, communicative, professional, and humorous. All of these traits also undergird a successful advising relationship (Delany et al., 2010).

Appreciative Advising

Appreciative advising, according to Damminger and Rakes (2017), draws from both developmental advising and the field of positive psychology. Emerging from appreciative inquiry used in organizational settings, this approach is gaining traction on college campuses (Damminger & Rakes, 2017). In creating a welcoming and supportive atmosphere, the advisor encourages the advisee to share his or her dreams and to move beyond any self-limiting expectations. Appreciative advising was first promoted by Bloom, Hutson, and He (2008), who defined the approach as an intentional and collaborative practice in which an academic advisor posed open-ended questions that help students optimize their educational experiences, achieve their goals and fulfill their potential.

The six major components of appreciative advising include a genuine caring and a deep belief in the potential of each student, appreciating that advising gives one the tremendous privilege of supporting another's growth, accepting that one can always refine the craft of advising, remaining aware that students see their advisors as powerful figures and using that power carefully and ethically, having a genuine interest in students and being open to learning from them, and being a culturally competent advisor (Bloom et al., 2008, p. 32).

Damminger and Rakes (2017) note that the advisor begins by asking students to share important information about themselves, what their dreams are, who their role models are, and what they view as their strengths, accomplishments, and life-changing experiences. From there, the advisor moves through the six phases of the advising process. Each phase contains unique tasks to be accomplished by both parties. In the first stage, "disarm," the advisor creates a welcoming environment, personalized by sharing some aspects of him or herself and setting the stage for a relationship that can grow and flourish over time (Damminger & Rakes, 2017). The goal is for the advisor to establish critical rapport and to allow the student into his or her world.

Welcoming and supportive non-verbal behavior, if sensitive to the norms and nuances of different cultures, can help invite the advisee into the relationship. Appreciating advising is a narrative approach, as Bloom et al. (2008) points out, and its primary aim is to "build trust and rapport with students via proper self-disclosure, invite students to make personal connections, and model storytelling that encourages students to share" (p. 40). Without authenticity on the advisor's part, this cannot take place. Advisees are asked to share stories that highlight their assets, so that they begin with recognition of talents and abilities that they bring to the college campus (Bloom et al., 2008).

The second phase, the "discover phase," relies on the use of positive, open-ended questions that assist students in locating and sharing their talents, strengths, and passions (Damminger & Rakes, 2017). These are questions that invoke story telling on the student's part, and in hearing those stories, the advisor learns more about the student as an individual so that s/he can help him or her articulate the assets that have been used to master challenges or solve problems in the past.

The "dream" phase requires that advisors shift from developing genuine relationships set in positive environments and move instead to understanding what the goals, aspirations, and dreams of each advisee are (Damminger & Rakes, 2017). This guidance permits students to envision a positive mental image of their future. The advisor can also guide the student towards career paths and academic majors that best match up with these dreams and that mesh well with the student's passions and talents.

In the "design" phase, the advisor-advisee team co-designs a future plan that results in the actualization of the advisee's dream (Damminger & Rakes, 2017). Advisors rely on goal-setting and concrete information to empower the student to make his or her freely-chosen decisions. Advisors also act in the networking role, making referrals to other individuals and campus/community resources that can help the student achieve the dream.

The "deliver" phase involves keeping the student on track to accomplish his/her goals (Damminger & Rakes, 2017). This means providing positive feedback when small goals are accomplished and advice about strategies that can help the advisee avoid pitfalls or master challenges that may be encountered. The advisor diligently tracks the student's progress and is there with guidance if the advisee decides to change course along the way.

Damminger and Rakes (2017) describe the "don't settle" phase as a challenge to students to raise their self-expectations. If a powerful partnership has been built, the advisor may see untapped potential in the advisee that s/he can't see in him or herself. In those instances, the advisor can carefully nudge the advisee out of his or her comfort zone to meet a larger challenge (Damminger & Rakes, 2017). This nudging can pay off when the student has faith in the advisor and has developed faith in self that is internalized over the course of the relationship.

Some institutions have adopted a different approach to appreciative advising; for example, the University of North Carolina (Greensboro campus) now integrates appreciative advising into all services to new arrivals on campus and probationary students. Staff have created a course that uses the six phases of the theory and have trained advisors to work specifically with students who have left the University and now are re-entering. Their research found that 90% of these students who signed a contract to meet with an appreciative advisor were academically eligible to continue their studies as opposed to only 33% of the control group (Habley, Bloom, & Robbins, 2012).

Employing Motivational Interviewing in the Advising Setting

Motivational interviewing (MI) is an incredibly valuable approach directly borrowed from counseling practice (Hughey & Pettay, 2013). It can help advisors move their advisees beyond ineffective ingrained habits such as procrastination, negotiating roles with significant others, time management, the inevitable roadblocks that college presents, and the fear of abandoning more comfortable roles for new growth (Hughey & Pettay, 2013). Motivational interviewing springs from one theorist whose optimistic, client-centered concept stressed people's capabilities for exercising free choice and changing through the process of self-actualization (Hughey & Pettay, 2013).

In good MI and advising, a truly egalitarian partnership must exist. Hughey and Pettay (2013) see MI as a collaborative partnership with the goal of developing motivation and implementing strategies to effect personal change; yet this partnership must be based on the four general principles of (a) expressing empathy, (b) developing discrepancy, (c) rolling with resistance, and (d) supporting self-efficacy (Hughey & Pettay, 2013). This approach requires the advisor to be directive in attempts to get the advisee to formulate motivational statements aimed towards his or her growth and change. This can be somewhat stressful for both parties, as it necessitates creating in the advisee an awareness of the discrepancy between his or her current state and the desired state (Hughey & Pettay, 2013; Miller & Rollnick, 2012). Such an awareness is dissonant in nature, which does not always feel good to the advisee.

Developing this discrepancy is exactly what forces the advisee to see that his/her present situation isn't consonant with his/her values or will not bolster the chances of achieving stated goals (Miller & Rollnick, 2012). Successful advisors will learn to tolerate the advisee's resistance, refraining from arguing with him or her if there is no desire for change (Miller & Rollnick, 2012). Since meaningful change can only come from someone who wishes to change, the advisor must wait until the moments of clarity when the student can perceive the incompatibility between present choices and articulated goals and values. This approach requires that the advisor serve in the capacity of information provider or observer, and only the advisee can be the change agent (Hughey & Pettay, 2013). When situations are stalled and not working to the student's benefit, this may be an excellent tactic to prompt change.

Once the advisor-advisee alliance has been formed, the advisor keeps a constant focus on the positive aspects of the advisee's progress. This is an essential element of MI because it conditions the advisee in the pursuit of his or her goals, develops a positive mindset, and is constantly focusing on the positive side of things. Utilizing open questions, affirmation, reflective listening, and summary reflections (OARS), the advisor builds a repertoire of techniques and skills in the process; the advisor uses these early and often," in the motivational interviewing approach (Miller & Rollnick, 2012). While this approach does not constitute an actual advising approach in and of itself, it is an extremely useful tool for situations in which advisees seem locked in attitudes and behaviors that are not moving them forward towards their stated goals.

Intrusive or Proactive Advising
Damminger & Rakes (2017) write that proactive advising is that which is comprised of intentional, well-timed communications with students in hopes of avoiding problems or at least responding early with the advice and resources necessary to prevent problems from being exacerbated. Proactive advising emerged from research that demonstrated the strong link between retention to graduation and a relationship with even just one member of the college campus that the student deemed important. Varney (2013) believes that retention is dependent upon implementing strategies to engage students and help them find that connection with their college community. Proactive advisors can serve this critical role because they can act as the vehicle between their advisees and various constituents of the college.

Varney (2007) reminds us that all colleges have at-risk students, and these are the very students that intrusive advising aims to reach before they drop out or are placed on academic probation. Intrusive advising is about getting to the heart about what really is causing a student's difficulties and arriving at an appropriate intervention before it is too late (Earl, 1987). This is an action-oriented approach that works alongside a student to assist him or her in accessing services and programs that can build skills and motivation to persist.

Glennen (1975) is credited as being the "father" of intrusive, or proactive advising; his core concepts were to provide students with information they needed before they actually asked for it and to use each individual's interests, assets and personal goals as the foundation of a relationship intended to boost persistence to graduation. In early studies, volunteer advisors, trained as proactive advisors, reviewed data on their advisees to build an early identification system for those who were deemed at-risk for failure due to a number of criteria (Glennen, 1975). Using this model, the retention rate improved among fragile students (Glennen, 1975). While some argue that college students should not need this kind of intrusive approach, others argue that the increasing numbers of underprepared students matriculating into a variety of campus cultures necessitates proactive advising for many, if not all, populations (Glennen, 1975).

Proactive advising requires deliberate intervention to enhance student motivation; using strategies to show interest and involvement with students; intensive advising designed to increase the probability of student success; working to educate students on all options; and approaching students before situations develop (Varney, 2013). Advisors contact their students prior to enrollment and are in continuous contact in order to monitor progress. While they still need to establish genuine relationships with each unique student, they also are very clear in terms of the rules, policies and protocols of the institution, as well as the advising relationship. In some cases, they may even develop contracts or other customized agreements with their students.

As with appreciative advising, advisors using this model will ask students to identify potential challenges in their education before they occur; doing so allows the dyad to strategize about how they will approach those barriers should they encounter them. Advisors are "intrusive" in that they usually require regular contact from their mentees; lack of follow through or engagement on the student's part will result in actions to re-establish steps towards goal attainment.

Damminger & Rakes (2017) view intrusive advising as a combination of developmental advising and proscriptive advising and "requires extensive advisor commitment, close monitoring of student progress, frequent student sessions that include assigned tasks, relevant referrals, and vigilant attention to uncovering stumbling blocks to student success" (p. 33).

Integrative Theory

Church (2005) reviewed all of the aforementioned theories, along with NACADA's six responsibilities of academic advisors and their core values statement. It was found that no theory had a clear-cut advantage over others in terms of a choice for an advisor, but that a fusion of aspects of each had merit at certain times and/or with certain students at various points in their academic career. Church (2005) articulated five components of integrative advising theory that he believed represented best practice in advising.

This theory began with the National Academic Advising Association (NACADA) Core Values and included ethical components such as beneficence, nonmaleficence, autonomy and fidelity (Church, 2005). The latter are ethical traits proposed by Kitchener (2000) that cover doing good for one's advisees, doing no harm, respecting free will and free choice, and honesty and trustworthiness.

Prescriptive advising is necessary to convey important information about curriculum and college protocols (Church, 2005). A focus on a well-rounded education, central to developmental advising, is also a component of the theory. Church (2005) also added reductive advising, in which the advisor focuses on identifying career goals and interests and arranges course schedules to reflect those. The final addition to this advising model is student approval as without fidelity to the student's free will and choices, the process is lost (Church, 2005). Using this multi-pronged approach, the author argues, results in an enjoyable college experience that ends with the student having met his or her goals, prepared for a chosen career, and well-rounded as a human being.

Advising with a Socratic Self-Examination Approach

Kuhtmann (2005) proposed a model of academic advising that aimed to incorporate 'quasi-Socratic' activities into the process of advising students over the lifespan of their studies. Called the 'beneficial dialectic,' the method allowed advisors to consider each advisee's level of development, interests, and learning environments as the relationship unfolds over the course of the program of study (Kuhtmann, 2005). The basic premise for this advising stance is that students can take control of their academic lives through reasoning, by engaging in dialogue with the advisor over their educational, career and personal goals for their college education and which courses and learning activities might best promote them (Kuhtmann, 2005).

Using a model that is vested in getting advisees to take more and more ownership over their academic choices, advisors pose questions that, through answering, the advisee eventually arrives at the desired knowledge (Kuhtmann, 2005). The advisor also asks students to become gradually more adept at providing a rationale and evidence for his or her choices. The level of dialogue takes into account a student's level of cognitive development over time, thus requiring that the advisor get to know his or her advisees well. It must also take into account a student's way of making meaning of his or her experiences, which may have cultural, gendered, or other roots.

Some feminist and cultural scholars have argued that the pure Socratic method of questioning feels alienating to women and those from more collective cultures; this can be counterbalanced by a relational approach in advising in which the advisor never seeks to upstage the advisee but acts as one who encourages student participation and expression, legitimizing their stories and opinions (Kuhtmann, 2005). The advisor may also practice beneficial dialectic with small groups of advisees, asking them to engage in true dialogue with one another rather than talking at each other (Kuhtmann, 2005).

Partners in this kind of dialogue exhibit particular characteristics that utilize a line of questioning and dialogue to help each member of the advising process arrive at useful self-reflection and clarification of goals (Kuhtmann, 2005). The characteristics (whether in an advisor-advisee dyad or group) include a true desire to investigate a matter, allowing an opportunity for all to speak and be heard, posing questions that facilitate mutual understanding, reflecting or mirroring one another's words, making one's viewpoints as clear as possible, being willing to give up an argument in the face of lack of evidence to support it, being open to investigating differences of opinion, and striving to arrive at consensus.

Kuhtmann (2005) wrote that advisors needed specific training in these methods and must be allowed the time to develop true relationships with advisees so that they have the level of awareness of students' individual needs, interests, and developmental phases necessary for good advising. In institutions where research and publication take precedence over advising and teaching, it is unlikely that such a model can be implemented successfully; however, when advisors are afforded the time and training to develop the beneficial dialectic approach through relational and communal means of advising, advisees can be helped to become authors and architects of their own college educational paths (Kuhtmann, 2005).

The Role of Advisor in Student Mental Health

Advisors and mentors are increasingly becoming de facto cogs in the mental health screening process on contemporary campuses (Kadison & DiGeronimo, 2004). A recent study found that 52% of college students responding reported feeling hopeless and 39% said they were so depressed that their functionality had been impaired some time during the past year (Eiser, 2015). Their report also documents a 2010 national survey of counseling center directors, who note sharp increases in clients with eating disorders, self-injury issues, and alcohol abuse (Eiser, 2015).

Burke et al. (2017, p. 129) quote two recent national studies that indicate 94% of counseling center directors are seeing an increase in students with severe psychological problems and 86% see more students entering college on psychiatric medications. While these were based on self-reports, and the increase in the past decade has not been huge, this still places advisors and other college personnel on the lookout for instances in which they may see students in distress and be able to make meaningful referrals for them if they have developed close ties. All good advising, as Wicks (2018) states, is relational and collaborative, and these elements are more critical than ever when coming to mental health interventions.

Sternberg (2018) quotes a Yale University professor, who developed the wildly-popular psychology course "Psychology and the Good Life," as saying: "College students are so much more overwhelmed, much more stressed, much more anxious, and much more depressed than they've ever been. I think we really have a crisis writ large at colleges in how students are doing in terms of self-care and mental health" (p. 22). Harper and Peterson (2015) reveal that faculty and staff see complex and clinical issues more often among students they teach and advise. In an infrequent study of graduate student mental health, Hyun, Quinn, Madon, and Lustig (2006) found mental health issues such as anxiety, depression, and a sense of isolation were key factors in students leaving college.

Burke et al. (2017) repeat the motto that "college should be challenging, not overwhelming" (p. 128). A certain degree of stretching outside of one's comfort zone is a necessary precursor to growth, but too much can lead to distress, exhibited in myriad ways. The authors caution that beliefs about mental health, willingness to seek help, acceptance of certain forms of treatment, and even presenting symptoms of a mental health issue may vary widely due to factors such as gender, cultural background, ethnicity and other factors.

While college advisors obviously are not trained to be clinical counselors, their relationships with their advisees can provide insightful views into students' mental and emotional health (Hyun et al., 2006). Advisors can build student resiliency through a variety of advising approaches. They can buffer their advisees from stress, anxiety, and loneliness through meaningful interactions and support; Hyun et al. (2006) found mentoring and advising to be protective against these conditions. These same authors reported that a student's relationship with his/her advisors was a salient factor in mental health, with dysfunctional relationships exacerbating mental health issues (Hyun et al., 2006).

Students who had a strong, positive relationship with their advisors were more likely to maintain positive mental health and wellbeing because when they suffered stress or anxiety, they were more apt to seek the advice or the help of advisors (Hyun et al., 2006). Advisors who knew their students well as individuals were more able to make effective referrals to appropriate resources when student needs fell outside of their levels of expertise or comfort (Hyun et al., 2006).

The best advisors are those who already have formed alliances with key resources on campus. Since this is a time in history when more students with disabilities and mental health issues (both identified and unidentified) are enrolling, advisors need to have vital connections with counseling and mental health centers, disability offices, and other campus health programs. It is also important to have an informal knowledge of the potential benefits of other activities, such as yoga, meditation, nutritional counseling, and stress management, which may be offered as non-credit, credit-bearing or other kinds of courses and educational experiences (Hyun et al., 2006).

Advisor Health and Well-Being

Teaching and advising are roles that can result in emotional wear and tear on faculty and advisors. A key to good advising practice is recognizing the demands of the contemporary post-secondary environment. Burke et al. (2017) note that those working on college campuses today are often subject to competing demands, work long hours, are often criticized or are not recognized for their contributions, and may be expected to fill many informal roles that are not necessarily part of their formal job description. This can lead to an imbalance in work-life configurations and difficulty in disengaging from the helping role.

The authors urge all advisors to think about how to recharge by staying cognizant of their own needs, monitoring their stress levels, and practicing self-care. Without doing so, they endanger their own emotional and physical health and cannot provide effective levels of care for others. Burke et al. (2017) cite an interesting model for a personal wellness plan that recognizes a multi-faceted definition of self. This can help the professionals understand that s/he needs to attend to the creative self, social self, coping self, spiritual self, and physical self in order to be a healthy individual (Burke et al., 2017).

Institutions of higher education would do well to devote professional development time and resources to promoting better health among their staff. In addition to professional development, incentives should be offered as a way to encourage the use of facilities, programs, and professionals who are employed to promote student well-being (Burke et al., 2017). Discussions of the state of one's health are an important collegial conversation at multiple institutional levels so that all personnel are highly functioning and can model high levels of commitment to self-care to students.

Advising Special Populations

A key element of a captivating campus is that all individuals and groups feel equal membership and equally valued on campus (Tomasiewicz, 2017). While that is a lofty goal for any institution, advisors can play a monumental role in welcoming special populations into the campus community and assisting them in recognizing the unique cultural treasures they can add to that community. Historically, special populations were defined as those marginalized in higher education settings who faced additional barriers to successful transition and completion of college (Tomasiewicz, 2017).

As campuses become more diverse, the categories of special populations have expanded to include low-income, first-generation, foreign, new immigrant, disabled, active service or retired military, members of the LGBTQ community, adult learners, and many others (Tomasiewicz, 2017). Recent definitions have even expanded to such populations as college athletes, women in math and sciences, commuters, transfer students, or ESL students. At this time in history, notes Tomasiewicz (2017), the working definition of special populations "describes any student cohort with either visible or invisible qualities or needs that may significantly affect the transition to college and attainment of academic goals" (p. 128).

Tomasiewicz (2017) cautions that many students will straddle or hold membership in a number of these groups. They may feel congruence with these groups' identities or diverge from one or more. This makes advising more complex, as the advisor cannot assume that because a student holds a group membership on paper, s/he feels a connection to that group. Some students may try to shed previous definitions as they come to campus; for example, many students with learning disabilities forego identifying with this status and hope to succeed without supports or group affiliation, although they often are not successful (Newman, & Madaus, 2015). Since a major part of matriculating at college is coming to a new sense of self, or at least initially reflecting upon one's previous cultural heritage and identities, an advisor must try to ascertain an advisee's sense of self in the here and now (Tomasiewicz, 2017).

For those students who fall into special populations categories, there are often additional concerns that have the potential to interfere with their success, especially during the transition and first-year college experience. Advisors can be on the look-out for signs of student distress. The first concern is what Davis (2010) calls 'imposter phenomenon.' This is far more serious than simply having concerns about fitting in and the phenomenon may exist either when things on campus are going well or going badly. Often imposters feel as though they have somehow taken the seat of a worthier student, have been admitted to college by mistake, or have achieved success (grades, praise, recognition) because college personnel are being kind, feel sorry for them, or are using strategies disingenuously to manage the classroom (Davis, 2010).

They may believe that their comments are not worthy of being shared in class or that their experiences are not relevant; such feelings can lead to anxiety, invisibility, and isolation.

Sakulku & Alexander's (2011) research on the imposter phenomenon illustrates how this condition can derail the academic plans of even the brightest students as even though high achieving women had objective evidence of their success, they were overcome with feelings of anxiety, fear of failure, and intellectual fraud (Sakulku & Alexander, 2011).

It is not uncommon among special populations for imposter phenomenon to lead a student down two different paths, neither of which was functional in college. The first was over-preparation and overworking, which could lead to exhaustion and even emotional breakdown, while the second path was procrastination and possible disengagement altogether (Sakulku & Alexander, 2011). In either case the cycle looked the same; upon achieving a goal, the student experienced a temporary feeling of relief, followed by discounting the positive feedback from advisors, faculty or others; s/he then cycled back into the feelings of perceived fraudulence or increased self-doubt, depression, and/or anxiety (Sakulku & Alexander, 2011).

Another possible impediment derives from social belonging theory in which advisors can encourage students to feel a sense of belonging within the college at large, or subgroups such as academic majors, clubs or service organizations; they build student resilience and lessen the likelihood of isolation or feeling as though one is not a full member of the college community (Walton & Cohen, 2011). Advisors of students who are from minority populations on campus can help these students build connections to resources or campus or community organizations, make introductions to other students who are succeeding in college, and match students with mentors who have come from similar backgrounds (Tomasiewicz, 2017).

Stereotype threat can hamper the success of special populations, as well. Such threats are based upon risks of confirming negative stereotypes about one's group, such as believing that women do not do well in math and the hard sciences (Tomasiewicz, 2017). Even the fear of confirming a stereotype can be enough to interfere with a student's performance or steer him or her away from academic choices that may be a good fit. Stereotype threat is powerful enough to negatively influence student performance in both academic and social spheres (Tomasiewicz, 2017). Advisors who are not familiar with how to help combat this threat can benefit from reviewing research.

Effective advising with these populations draws heavily upon the cultural competencies developed in the counseling field (Sue et al., 1982). The end result of culturally competent counseling (and advising) is to be able "to work with others who are culturally different from self in meaningful, relevant, and productive ways" (Sue et al., 1982, p. 13). These fall into three identified categories to include knowledge, skills, and awareness (Sue et al., 1982).

College advisors need to begin with an awareness of both their own cultural values, beliefs and attitudes, as these may affect how they perceive and interact with students from cultures different from their own (Holder, 2013). They also need to have an awareness of other cultures, but within this awareness, they also need to recognize the divergence of different subcultures within a larger culture so that they do not assume homogeneity (Holder, 2013). This is difficult work and requires individual and institutional development over time.

Multicultural knowledge is the second component of Sue et al.'s (1982) models. This involves increasing an individual's knowledge of cultural traditions, values, histories, and practices over time; travel; relationships with others; learning from personal advisees; and formal study (Sue, 2001). This also involves reflection upon personal cultural viewpoints, and how these may influence interactions with others is a critical skill in understanding what an advisor brings to the table in initial contacts with students who may come from other backgrounds (Sue et al., 1982).

Howard-Hamilton (2000) describes culturally-competent advisors as having the following attributes and practicing the following behaviors:

- being comfortable with personal racial identity and cultural identity (ies);
- understanding personal biases and checking assumptions;
- willing to ask questions about diversity while suspending judgement;
- understanding the limits of one's own cultural understanding and not being afraid to consult with advisees;
- creating a climate that promotes dialogue, disagreement, reflection, challenge and support;
- developing realistic goals with advisees; following up with advisees;
- engaging in multicultural learning and professional development; and consulting with a multiculturally competent mentor.

Many of the skills involved in culturally competent counseling are the same that comprise any effective counseling relationship. These include establishing rapport, having genuine positive regard for the advisee, and practicing non-judgmental listening; however, there is another layer of skills that are linked to cultural knowledge of both verbal and non-verbal communication, recognition of cultural makeup and possible biases of an institution, current events, and biases and prejudices at a national level (Holder, 2013). This is a great deal of information to be gleaned and processed, and many advisors with a more traditional viewpoint may feel that this is beyond the scope or definition of their role. A campus that creates an environment that captivates all members must build community out of an appreciation for diversity, however hard that work may be (Holder, 2013).

Archambault (2015) proposed five seminal questions to build an advisor's exploration of cultural competence in advising. They include

- asking how the student's experience might differ from the advisor's;
- whether the advisor might be making any assumptions about the student based upon visible and invisible aspects of diversity;
- whether assumptions about students on campus fit a particular advisee;
- what characteristics contribute to student success or challenges on campus; and
- what internal (personal) assets and institutional assets does the advisee possess that can be brought to bear on his/her education?

This set of questions can prime an advising session for a more open approach to seeing the advisee in his/her unique entirety and may prompt the advisor into further reflection upon his/her own background, assumptions, and need for further cultural knowledge.

Fleming, Coffman, and Harter (2006) urge advisors to conduct what they call 'environmental scans.' This entails trying to view the institution and its component parts from the viewpoint of students, and a diverse group of students; for example, those who have disabilities, those who are from a cultural minority, an adult or commuter student. This includes a sense of the classroom environment as well as the non-academic environment and the surrounding community. Attending campus events, eating in the dining commons, seeing when offices are open and how they bundle services for student convenience are all ways to get more familiar with the culture of a campus from a student's eye view.

Developing a skill in advising any student who might walk into one's office can be a daunting task, but as Tomasiewicz (2018) stresses

> *All advisors bear responsibility for understanding the whole of each student in need of advising. Therefore, each advisor must prepare for any student encounter and continually develop the cultural competencies and critical consciousness necessary to offer effective assistance to students seeking to meet educational goals* (p. 143).

Advising Online Students

While online students are at a higher risk for isolation and other deterrents to feeling fully connected to the campus community, effective advising bridge these gaps. Some advisors find it challenging to provide the same high quality advising that they do to students with whom they can have regular, face-to-face interactions (Ohrablo, 2018; Young, Jean, & Quayson, 2017). Ohrablo (2018) reports on research finding that many advisors who are used to traditional advising modes may not experience goodness of fit in online or low residency models that they experience as a more disconnected, labor-intensive method of advising; they also may struggle to integrate the same developmental approaches they traditionally used in their advising models.

While the reasons for choosing online study may have to do with learning style preferences, geographic restraints, or life responsibilities, online students have the same developmental needs as others (Young, Jean, & Quayson, 2017). The trick is in how to create meaningful advising relationships. In the informational role, advisors may need to be more proactive in their outreach to students. While campus-based students can walk into offices or one-stop centers, it can be frustrating to gain important information and make office contact when studying totally online (Ohrablo, 2018). Advisors can bridge this gap by using calls, email, video or group advising sessions using various technologies to impart need to know information such as curriculum, registration procedures, policies, campus resources, and contact information (Young, Jean, & Quayson, 2017).

The trick in online advising, Ohrablo (2018) notes, is to create a parallel experience to what students would be provided if they were advised individually or in a small group in the office. This includes not only giving important information but also discovering who students are as individuals, learners, and career aspirants. Additionally, advisors want to establish rapport through sharing some of their own background and interests as part of the welcome stage of the relationship.

Gordon, Levinson, and Kirkner (2018) and Ohrablo (2018) caution against overwhelming these students with too much information at any one time. Advisors must strike a delicate balance between being proactive with information that students need but doing it in a developmentally appropriate way, on a need to know basis, so that information is chunked and manageable but arrives prior to being needed so that students do not miss out on steps in required processes and protocols. One way to do this efficiently is to develop targeted mass communications in which only the students who need particular information receive it, while still including the advisees.

Given that online students may be scattered all over the country or globe, synchronous (real time, live) advising often poses some unique challenges (Gordon et al., 2018). Phone calls, based upon students' availability and preferences, can be set up at mutually-convenient times and indicate to the students that their advisor cares about meeting their needs. Effective phone advising, which can be threatened by poor connectivity and environmental distractions, must find a way to simulate the critical elements of in-person advising (such as body language and other non-verbal cues).

If students only receive mass communications, they miss out on the most critical part of advising - the human connection, encouragement, modeling, and networking that advisors provide (Gordon et al., 2018). Students need to feel connected to a real person who cares about their success, knows them as an individual, understands their goals for college, and can help them locate resources (both human and other) that can help them attain those goals. They also need encouragement in times of doubt or struggle, as well as empathy during personal trials. Finally, one of the most valuable assets an advisor has is the ability to make connections for his or her advisees; this may mean putting them in touch with peers who share similar interests, other faculty, potential mentors, or community resources (Ohrablo, 2018).

The trick to good online advising is to take each of the advising approaches mentioned and think about how to translate it into modes other than face-to-face; for example, proactive or intrusive online advising may mean regular, advisor-initiated check-ins, whether the student has reached out or not (Starks, 2015). Motivational interviewing techniques may be as valuable when conducted in a phone or video session. Following up with online students who the advisor knows may be having personal or family difficulties is just as meaningful if heartfelt. Academic success and retention of online students, as well as advisor satisfaction, are achieved when advisors find equivalent ways of duplicating the techniques and strategies they find useful and personally meaningful in campus-based endeavors (Starks, 2015).

Best Practices for College Campuses

Kuh (2006) writes that there are four common themes among quality advising programs on college campuses. The first is that advisors know their students well and that they subscribe to a talent development perspective on education. Of course, this means that institutions must create advising loads of reasonable numbers of students and provide time and resources for this knowledge to be gleaned. Second, mentor-mentee relationships are close and meaningful, again entailing that ratios be manageable. Successful programs also begin with early connections with advisors, and advisors are involved in planning and delivering orientation and other first-year or transition experiences (Kuh, 2006).

Advisors in these programs make a point of connecting classroom learning to life situations, always helping their advisees identify paths to academic and social success. This brings them to suggest co-curricular experiences that are appropriate for each advisee, including service learning, travel abroad, internships, clubs, community activities, and experiential learning. In many cases, advisors also assist advisees in acculturation processes, such as learning the traditions, rituals and protocols that define campus life (Kuh, 2006).

On high-performing campuses, Kuh et al., (2005b) reveals, advising and student success are a "tag team" activity, forming early alert and support teams across a number of roles and offices. Because of coordination of personnel and activities, it is far less likely that any one student can fall through the cracks of the institution.

Participants in a study on advising and mentoring by Michael and Wilkins (2014) had plenty of advice for institutions to include hiring faculty who see mentoring as necessary to their role. Beyond hiring the right faculty, there should be explicit training in the art of advising/mentoring (Michael & Wilkins, 2014). Faculty mentors need to be reminded that their enthusiasm for the student and his/her interests is a motivating factor (Michael & Wilkins, 2014).

Even though participants were graduate students, they believed that all first-year students should have a high quality mentor to support them (Michael & Wilkins, 2014). Mentors should first model behaviors and expectations and created structures that give newbies a sense of comfort and security (Michael & Wilkins, 2014). Given that many programs are online, hybrid, or low-residency, mentoring must take many forms, and each must be a just-right fit for the student. Good advisors/mentors go beyond the scholastic realm of their roles and serve as social connectors between their students and the wider campus (Michael & Wilkins, 2014).

In addition to advice from study participants, institutions need to provide faculty with quality professional development and training in the art of advising/mentoring (Pinto, 2018). This needs to be expanded from traditional academic departmental orientations to broad-range presentations and discussions of the various theories of advising. There needs to be greater emphasis on the mental health aspects of advising/mentoring, as well, with a special emphasis on how effective mentoring can prevent or ameliorate the stress of academia (Pinto, 2018).

While faculty are trained to see their primary and most clearly articulated role as an advisor to provide assistance and guidance in purely academic endeavors, "a greatly under-appreciated role of effective advisors is to provide psychological support, guidance, and assistance to students who are often working through some of the most difficult periods in their lives, both personally and professionally. The amount of time involvement advisors spend in the personal lives of students is a matter of choice, but if they choose not to take an active role in helping students with mental health issues they at least need to know how to recognize problems and have resources to point students toward" (Turley, 2013, n.p.).

Institutions that value advising and mentoring will elevate their recognition of that aspect of the professoriate through awards, professional development opportunities, and research grants. Advising can be a part of ongoing discussion in annual faculty evaluations; faculty should be encouraged to talk about their advising experiences, including identifying resources they might need to better support their mentoring (Turley, 2013).

Final Thoughts

College personnel have a powerful role to play beyond teaching content in the classroom or fulfilling their specific role requirements; while many hold formal roles as academic advisors, still others assume informal advising roles as students reach out for connections and information. Advising alone cannot influence many things on campus; it can't directly change the curriculum, administrative decisions, fiscal exigencies, or extra-curricular offerings. Yet, it is an avenue for creating the kinds of human connections that students need. As this paper has demonstrated, the field of advising has moved from a traditional stance in which formal advising centered on academic matters to a more multi-faceted definition of the role, combining best practices from academic, career, and personal counseling.

Contemporary advisors/mentors work with a multitude of factors (academics, career goals, social connections, peer relationships, family obligations, financial status, and school-life balance) that influence student success. Sometimes nurturing, sometimes nudging, sometimes directly challenging, the advisor uses strategies mentioned above to guide advisees to the fullest expression of their potential possible. Institutions that place high value on advising and mentoring need to adopt stronger strategies to develop and reward high-quality advisors. These will include training and professional development, public recognition, and professional opportunities for study and research.

Skilled mentorship makes all the difference in a student's educational experience. This is equally true at both the graduate and undergraduate levels. A quality advisor/advisee relationship might include regular, meaningful contact that is both personal and academic; feedback that is both specific and timely; meeting other mentors and peers that could offer assistance; and a true personal touch.

Points to Remember

- *Advisors play a critical role in students' campus integration, personal development, persistence to graduation, and career preparation.*
- *Contemporary college advisors must move beyond traditional models of advising to more developmental ones that take a "whole student" approach.*
- *There are many effective models of student advising and the savvy advisor may need to use or integrate several of them in order to help advisees reach their academic, personal and career goals.*
- *All advisors, regardless of job title or responsibility, must be able to work effectively with special populations on campus.*
- *Given the growing diversity on American college campuses, advisors need to become culturally competent in their work, drawing on many concepts from multicultural counseling.*
- *Students desire opportunities to connect with their advisors in settings other than formal advising sessions.*
- *Institutions that truly understand the value of competent and caring advisors will make commitments of professional development, time, money and recognition for this invaluable role.*

Chapter Seven

Inviting and Potent Instruction:

Best Practices to Cultivate Learning

The most important attribute of teaching is the student, whether it be the 18-year-old first year student, the adult returning to the classroom, or the professional in a continuing education program (Preston, 2017). In an ever-changing society, educational professionals must pay attention to the emerging trends in order to meet the students where they are at and their unique educational needs (Preston, 2017).

Students are now entering the classroom expecting to both engage and be engaged (Preston, 2017). They are eager to learn, participate, and contribute; therefore, instructors must find the right means to motivate and keep them engaged (Preston, 2017). Viewing students as partners in learning allows instructors to give them more responsibility in contributing to the academic environment, the ability to interact with their peers, the opportunity to practice their new content and skills, and demonstrate their knowledge (Preston, 2017).

Partnerships between instructors and faculty also provide a unique opportunity for instructors to learn with and from their students (Preston, 2017). To meet students where they are at, and retain them as partners, instructors should capitalize on their breadth of knowledge and enthusiasm by sharing control and offering choices, ensuring that a student's experience will contribute to his or her long-term learning and become part of his or her life-long framework for living and understanding the world (Preston, 2017; Meyers, 2014).

Active Learning

Research and theory have both demonstrated that students learn through building their own knowledge and by connecting new ideas and experiences to existing knowledge and experiences to form fresh or enriched understanding (Brame, 2016). This active learning experience not only allows students to make connections between new information and their current mental models, but allows them to confront misconceptions (Brame, 2016). Active learning activities that students can do themselves to construct knowledge and understanding include group projects, presentations, participation in discussions in and out of class, participation in community-based or service-learning projects, and tutoring peers (Brame, 2016; Meyers, 2014). Although these activities vary, they all require students to perform higher order thinking and metacognitive operations that promote self-reflection (Brame, 2016).

Strategies to Actively Engage Students in Lectures

The Pause Procedure

While lecturing, instructors should pause for two minutes every 12 to 18 minutes to encourage students to discuss and rework notes in pairs or teams, promoting a review of their understanding of the lecture material and its organization. This brief period of time also allows students chances to frame questions or receive clarification, both of which significantly increase their learning (Brame, 2016).

Retrieval

To prompt students to retrieve information from memory, thus improving a student's long-term memory and ability to learn subsequent material, instructors should pause for two or three minutes every 15 minutes of lecture to have students write all they can remember from the preceding class segment (Brame, 2016; Millis, 2010).

Demonstrations

Before a demonstration, students should predict the results and discuss their prediction with a peer. After a demonstration and before the instructor's explanation, students should discuss the observed result and how it may have differed from their prediction. This method allows students to test their understanding of a system by predicting an outcome, and if the prediction is incorrect, allows them to see any misconceptions they may have had (Brame, 2016).

Think-Pair-Share

This method of active learning involves asking students a question that requires higher order thinking and has them think or write about an answer for one minute, then discuss their responses with a peer for two minutes. Responses can then be shared to allow students the opportunity to critically consider other responses and help students articulate newly formed mental connections (Millis, 2010).

Peer Instruction & Concept Questions

This method is a modification of think-pair-share and involves personal response devices such as clickers or an online application. Professors should pose a conceptually based multiple-choice question and ask students to contemplate an answer and vote on a response using a polling system such as a clicker or online application. Using this method can promote active participation and engagement, particularly for those students who are shy about participating in class-wide discussions (Bruff, 2017; Lutes, 2016).

Once the students have voted, they can discuss their answer with a nearby classmate. Students should be encouraged to change their answer after a discussion if they feel this is necessary. Class voting results may then be shared via a graph of student responses to stimulate further discussion (Brame, 2016; Lutes, 2016).

Minute Papers

Like think-pair-share, this approach encourages students to articulate and examine newly formed information by having them write for one minute about a question that requires them to reflect on their learning or to engage in critical thinking. Responses can be shared in class to stimulate discussion or collected and used to inform future class sessions (Lang, 2017).

Activities to Replace Lectures and Engage Students

Strip Sequence

To strengthen students' logical thinking processes and test their mental model of a process, instructors can give students the steps in a process on strips of paper that are jumbled and ask them to work together to reconstruct the proper sequence (Brame, 2016).

Concept Map

Concept maps are visual representations of the relationships between key concepts (Nowak & Govin, 1984). Students should determine, on their own or in small groups, the general relationship between concepts and arrange them two at a time, draw arrows between related concepts and label with a short phrase to describe the relationship (Brame, 2016). Once students can see visual representations of their own thinking processes, they can develop more sophisticated models that recognize that there may be more than one right answer to a problem (Brame, 2016).

Mini-Maps

Mini-maps are similar to concept maps except students usually have a relatively short list of specific terms to incorporate into their map, allowing them to be completed by groups more quickly (Brame, 2016).

Categorizing Grids

Students may be given a grid made up of several important categories and a list of scrambled terms, images, or equations to quickly sort into the correct categories in the grid. This approach can be particularly effective in assisting instructors to identify misconceptions that students may have shown when expressing the distinctions they made within a field of related items (Brame, 2016).

Student-Generated Test Questions

Instructors may provide students with a copy of their learning goals for a particular unit and challenge groups of students to create test questions that correspond to those goals. Students can then share their favorite test question, or all test questions can be shared with the whole class to serve as a potential study guide (Briggs, 2014; Meyers, 2014).

Decision-Making Activities

Providing students with the opportunity to imagine they are policy-makers who must make and justify tough decisions regarding real-world problems can help students critically consider a challenging problem and encourage them to be creative in considering solutions (Brame, 2016).

Case-Based Learning

Akin to decision-making activities, case-based learning presents students with real-world situations that require them to apply their knowledge to reach a conclusion about an open-ended situation (Meyers, 2014). When examining a case, students should decide what they know that is relevant, what other information is needed, and the potential impacts of their decisions (Brame, 2016).

Creating Assignments and Assignment Choice

To engage students in the classroom, readings, lectures, and in-class activities that help students focus can be designed by putting an emphasis on the search for answers, enabling students to be active in their own learning process (Armstrong & Stanton, 2017). Questions and activities can be designed that highlight the professional implications of what the students are being asked to do, making the material and work more meaningful and relevant (Armstrong & Stanton, 2017; Briggs, 2014).

Having deliberate discussions in the classroom on how the class itself and the assignments help students develop disciplinary or professional expertise also helps students develop metacognition skills (Armstrong & Stanton, 2017; Meyers, 2014). Being able to reflect on and analyze their own ways of thinking and learning will allow students to move beyond the idea that learning is something that happens to them and realize that their education is something they can actually create and control (Armstrong & Stanton, 2017).

Instructors can ensure continual student engagement in classroom activities and assignments by creating non-graded assignments where students are able to comment on their own work, describe their problem-solving process, and explain their chosen methods and techniques. By giving assignments in these ways, students will become producers of knowledge instead of mere consumers of knowledge (Armstrong & Stanton, 2017).

Allowing students to choose their own assignments may also help promote student engagement and investment in learning (Ferlazzo, 2017). Instructors can construct a list of potential assignments from which students must collectively decide, by majority vote, which ones they will be responsible for. The assignments should all have a definable learning purpose that is directly related to the course's learning goals, promote student buy-in, and demonstrate the real-life relevance of the subject matter (Ferlazzo, 2017).

Instructors may use assignments that have students find and summarize a relevant news story paragraph or write about a particular topic in class; for example, 'my favorite disease.' For each assignment, nominal point values and due dates should be assigned as well as a few critical questions that students must address in each paragraph, such as the source of the information, a summary of information in their own words, or to share something they learned about the subject they did not know before the assignment (Ferlazzo, 2017).

Just-in-Time Teaching

Just-in-Time Teaching (JiTT) is a teaching and learning strategy designed to promote the use of class time for more active learning that relies on a feedback loop between web-based learning materials and the classroom (Brame, 2018). When using this strategy, students prepare for class by reading from the textbook or other resources and complete assignments online. Answers to the assignments are sent to the instructor a few hours before class, allowing time for the instructor to adapt a lesson, if necessary, and create an interactive classroom environment that emphasizes active learning and cooperative problem solving (Brame, 2018).

Two often used, quick assignments are warm-ups and puzzles (Brame, 2018). Warm-ups are short, web-based assignments that are designed for students to complete before receiving any instruction on the topic, thus prompting students to think about the upcoming lesson so they are prepared to develop more complex answers in class (Brame, 2018). Using warm-ups also frees up class time to focus on clarifying specific responses and exploring areas where more help is needed (Brame, 2018). In turn, puzzles are short, web-based assignments that integrate concepts and wrap-up a session on a topic that has previously been covered in class (Brame, 2018).

The Peer Instruction Method

Research has demonstrated that the peer instruction method, compared to traditional lecture-based pedagogy, leads to more positive outcomes for students, teachers, institutions, and all disciplines as well (Schell & Butler, 2018). Peer instruction can result in lower failure rates, especially in challenging courses, higher retention rates in STEM majors, and a reduction of the gender gap in academic performance in science (Schell & Butler, 2018). Peer instruction allows students to develop more vigorous quantitative problem-solving skills, more accurate conceptual knowledge, increased academic self-efficacy, and an increased interest in and enjoyment of the subject (Bruff, 2017; Schell & Butler, 2018).

The peer instruction method involves a structured series of learning activities that aim to develop student interaction during class lectures and focus students' attention on underlying concepts (Schell & Butler, 2018). To start, instructors should focus students' attention by posing a conceptual question in a multiple-choice or short answer format with the remaining activities built off this question (Bruff, 2017; Schell & Butler, 2018).

Once the question has been posed to the students, they should have time to think and construct an answer based on their current understanding and then record and display their answers using a classroom response method, such as a clicker or online polling application (Schell & Butler, 2018; Lutes, 2016). Using high-tech systems have several benefits including the provision of anonymity and the ability for the instructor to review and analyze the answers at a later date and potentially modify his or her teaching plan (Schell & Butler, 2018; Lutes, 2016).

When all answers have been received, the instructor can review them without disclosing, displaying, or sharing the correct answer or the frequency of choices among the students (Bruff, 2017; Lutes, 2016). At this point, students can use reasoning to convince their neighboring peers that their answer is the correct one. If the student's neighbor has the same answer, instructors may direct students to find a peer with a different answer, so they have the opportunity to justify the reasoning behind their chosen answer, using knowledge that was previously heard, read, learned, or studied (Schell & Butler, 2018).

After adequate time for discussions, students have the opportunity to keep their same answer or change the answer. Once the decisions have been made, they can then record their final answer using the same response method they used for the original answer (Schell & Butler, 2018; Lutes, 2016). Instructors then reveal and explain the correct answer and display the pre-post response frequencies, so students may see how their answers changed and how many other students selected specific answers (Lutes, 2016).

By asking students to explain the rationale for their correct, or even incorrect, answer, allows students to interrogate and resolve any potential misconceptions that led them to choose an answer that served as a distractor (Schell & Butler, 2018). Having students explain the correct answer to their peers can be more effective than having the instructor explain as students, as novices, may be able to better communicate the information than the instructor as an expert in their field (Schell & Butler, 2018).

Small Teaching

A student's classroom learning experience can be divided into four parts to include the moment before class actually begins, the very opening moments of class, the middle section, which is greatest in length, and the closing moments (Lang, 2017). To increase student engagement prior to the start of class, instructors can project a picture onto the whiteboard that students will see while getting out their materials in preparation for class. This permits the faculty member to connect with his or her students at the beginning of class by asking them to express their observations involving the image (Lang, 2017).

During the first few minutes of class, instead of having the instructor review what happened in the prior class, they should ask students to remind them of what was covered, using questions that force students into the more sophisticated processes of reflecting and evaluating (Briggs, 2014; Lang, 2017). Helping students make fully-formed mental networks, and providing meaningfulness and relevancy keeps students from middle-of-the-class boredom and aids their long-term storage of information; this can be enhanced through the creation of connection notebooks that require the students to link what they are learning in class to the real world (Briggs, 2014; Lang, 2017).

Notebooks can be reviewed throughout a semester and can be a dedicated notebook, a regular notebook, posted online, or shared in small groups. Ideally, students should have an opportunity to write in the notebooks at least once weekly for every class they are enrolled in; the writing's value lies in having students answer instructor prompts that require students to articulate how course content is reflected in daily home or campus life, in readings, or in other media that the students experience outside of the classroom (Lang, 2017).

To capture students at the end of class when they are anxious to pack their bags and leave, instructors should establish a closing ritual that ensures learning will continue right through to the end of class and beyond. Writing minute papers or exit tickets that ask students to write about seminal information they learned in that day's class and what questions they still have, permits the quick retrieval practice that invites reflection and evaluation (Brame, 2016; Lang, 2017).

Flipped Classrooms: Teaching Inside-Out

Teaching class inside-out by making class content available online not only opens up more class time for students to apply material, solve problems, and analyze solutions, it places more responsibility on the students, which in turn keeps them more engaged (Richardson, 2017). Research has demonstrated that attention in class drops off significantly after the first few minutes of lecture. Making lecture content available outside of class can alleviate distractions such as texting, using social media apps, or even daydreaming (Richardson, 2017).

Posting lecture material on various media outlets or into a podcast allows instructors to differentiate instruction. Students can listen to the material at midnight, pause for an important point, review a troublesome concept, or even skip ahead (Richardson, 2017). This freedom to work at their own pace on their own schedule can result in students actually paying more attention to a larger portion of the material (Richardson, 2017; Young, Jean, & Quayson, 2017).

For those instructors who do not want to use social media, reading is still a viable option for delivering information, especially when context and questions are posed to the students. Students are more likely to take responsibility and accountability for reading the course material when the information is not subsequently repeated in a lecture (Nilson, 2017). Quick quizzes at the beginning of class will allow instructors to demonstrate that they are serious about the students' need to cover the material on their own and can have the added benefit of preventing tardiness and serving as a class attendance mechanism (Richardson, 2017).

To ensure students will actually buy the books and do the reading, instructors should make sure that the chosen reading material takes into consideration the average student's reading ability, contains graphics and pictures that reinforce the text, and pares the required pages to what is essential (Nilson, 2017). Instructors should also explain why the particular reading material was chosen, its purpose, value, and relevancy, and endeavor to make explicit connections between the material and in-class activities, written assignments, and exams (Nilson, 2017).

Most students are not familiar with how to read textbooks like an expert and need to be taught how to read with the purpose of gaining useful and important information. Instructors may wish to demonstrate the marginalia method to assist students in discerning the main points of an assigned reading (Nilson, 2017). Class time should be designated to cover a few pages of the reading in which students have the opportunity to underline any key phrases or words as well as write 3-5 words next to each paragraph that either summarizes or reacts to the content. Once this has been completed, students can be asked to justify their marginalia and underlining choices and compare them to those of the instructor (Nilson, 2017). Similarly, students can be asked to highlight with discernment and then compare what they have highlighted to what the instructor has highlighted, enabling them to learn the expert's reasoning for distinguishing certain parts of the text over others (Nilson, 2017).

With lecture material now being relegated to homework status, class time is freed up to provide the guidance and feedback students need to engage in transformative learning (Richardson, 2017). Instructors are now able to pose more challenging problems to the students that demand more critical thinking and have the time and ability to provide immediate feedback (Richardson, 2017). Research shows that learning is significantly enhanced when instructors are able to deliver frequent, timely, individualized feedback, use class time to answer questions, identify and clear up misconceptions, respond to performance, and evaluate arguments or evidence (Richardson, 2017).

Social Media

Research indicates that outside of going to a student's residence hall or running into them by chance and discussing course content, there is no other method that is as pervasive, cost-effective, or engaging as using social media to enhance student-student, student-faculty, and student-content engagement outside of class (Heiberger & Junco, 2017).

In order to meet students where they are at and, yet, keep course content decisions driven by educational pedagogy, social media can, and should, be incorporated into an instructor's curriculum design (Heiberger & Junco, 2017). Health science instructors, for example, may create and maintain a social networking page that shares the risks and precautions for specific medical conditions; whereas political science instructors might have students use a short message service (SMS) to keep abreast of breaking news and conduct out-of-class discussions related to current political issues (Heiberger & Junco, 2017). The use of social media also allows students to share links, answer questions from the instructor, and even pose questions to fellow students (Heiberger & Junco, 2017).

Instructors may also use social media outside of their formal learning environment to form a personal learning network in which they can post and converse with students and other educational professionals about interesting ideas and topics (Heiberger & Junco, 2017). Many professional conferences, for example, use an SMS hashtag before, during, and after the event so participants may discuss and share content, analyses, and reactions (Heiberger & Junco, 2017).

Final Thoughts

With the advent and increase in technology and social media, there is an increasing need for instructors to meet students where they are at. College students are entering classrooms expecting to engage, to be engaged, eager to learn, participate, and contribute. To minimize the distraction of technology and to provide much needed meaningfulness and relevancy, instructors must make the shift to view students as more than just students; they must be viewed as partners who are just as responsible for their education and learning environment as the instructor.

Conducting deliberate and purposeful classroom discussions and providing students with a choice in assignments will foster student engagement by providing students with the relevance, relatedness, and utility value they are seeking. Students will thus have a greater responsibility in their learning and, as a result, feel that learning is something more than something happening around or to them, but something they have an active and engaged role in.

Points to Remember

- *When students can choose content and method of study, they will become producers of knowledge, which increases their engagement over learning environments that relegate them to being simply consumers of others' created knowledge.*
- *The peer instruction method creates more positive outcomes for students, instructors, and institutions, as well as result in lower failure rates, higher retention rates in STEM majors, a reduction of the gender gap in academic performance in science, and increased academic self-efficacy, interest, and enjoyment.*
- *To meet the needs and interests of contemporary students, there is no other method that is as pervasive, cost-effective, or engaging as using social media to enhance student-to-student, student-to-faculty, and student-to-content engagement outside of the classroom.*

Chapter Eight

Beyond Academics: Enhancing the Educational Experience through Extracurricular Activities

The manner in which the majority of students learn best is through activities that fall outside of traditional classrooms. This fact must influence the mission of any college or university, as institutions of higher education bear the responsibility for developing the whole student and must create a menu of cocurricular activities that enhance a well-rounded education (Lau, Hsu, Acosta, & Hsu, 2013; Rutter & Mintz; 2016). Such extracurricular activities center on three different constituencies—the institution's students, the institution, and the larger community that surrounds the institution. Extracurricular activities both supplement the school's academic mission and round out the student's education more fully (Tenhouse, 2018).

Different from extracurricular activities, cocurricular activities intentionally align themselves with as well as augment and enhance standard curricular goals (Rutter & Mintz, 2016). Activities can either be embedded within existing academic programs, such as study abroad, undergraduate research experiences, and service learning, or they can be set apart from the curriculum, such as greenhouses and workshops (Rutter & Mintz, 2016).

For many students, participating in interesting and compelling extracurricular activities and/or cocurricular activities keeps them motivated and engaged (Lau et al., 2013). These opportunities are not only developmental, transformative, and future-focused, they offer authentic, hands-on opportunities to hone skills, put ideas into practice, and showcase achievements of potential interest to employers as well (Rutter & Mintz, 2016).

Extracurricular Activities

Student Government

Most higher education institutions have myriad opportunities for students to exert their positive leadership. In many cases, these leaders must win election against their peers; their main role is to act as a conduit or an official voice to university administrators and serve on campus-wide committees to bring their peers' ideas and concerns to the forefront (Tenhouse, 2018). Student government plays a fiscal role on campus by helping to disperse funds, developing programs that mirror student interests and needs, holding open forums for discussion and debate and connecting different student constituencies on campus to build cohesion and support for one another's agendas (Tenhouse, 2018). These activities can teach students elements of strategic planning, organizing, exerting ethical and sound leadership, and solving problems in new and creative ways (Lau et al., 2013).

Athletics

Intercollegiate and intramural or club sports are a highlight of most campus experiences. Participating in varsity athletics requires students to make a significant time commitment and focus their energy on practicing, conditioning, and competing (Tenhouse, 2018). Intramural sports, such as flag football, rugby, or tennis allow for a lesser level of competition and time commitment while providing some pressure and commitment; many students have developed their own competitions and sought funding for activities such as Ultimate Frisbee, hiking clubs, or camping and mountaineering expeditions (Tenhouse, 2018).

Professional and Academic Organizations

Organizations that are based on students' academic major or potential future profession serve as a link between academia and the professional real world and can assist students acquire knowledge and skills that aid them in moving towards future careers and employment (Tenhouse, 2018; Great Value Colleges, 2018). During organizational meetings, students become steeped in the relevant professional issues and learn job related skills that provide an orientation to the field (Tenhouse, 2018). Most academic professional organizations provide students with research-based resources and opportunities to attend skill building workshops taught by well-known industry leaders (Great Value Colleges, 2018).

Service-Related and Volunteer Activities

While volunteer and service-related activities have great benefit for students' experiential learning, they simultaneously benefit local and global communities through improving their locales and the lives of their citizens (Tenhouse, 2018). Service-learning programs, such as Habitat for Humanity, Big Brothers/Big Sisters, or Mentor give students the satisfaction of meaningful service, but are particularly valuable in opportunities for student reflection, individually or in groups, can be incorporated into the experiences (Hsu, Acosta, & Hsu, 2013; Tenhouse, 2018).

Multicultural Activities

Multicultural activities come in various forms; these might include ethnic fairs, celebrations, musical events or culinary feasts, as well as academic lectures, student panels, or guest speakers. The primary value to all involved is to step outside familiar boundaries and see the world through others' eyes. Those who take part in singular events or clubs or organizations that promote greater understanding of racial, ethnic, or sexual-identity issues are more likely to develop better cross-cultural competencies (Tenhouse, 2018). Participating in a club that promotes ethnic and national diversity will also enable students to gain a global perspective within a group setting and cultivate personal relationships, not strictly professional ones (Great Value Colleges, 2018).

Arts

The fine arts departments are venues for many extracurricular opportunities such as acting, singing in a musical, participating in marching band, or creating pottery and sculpture. These activities serve both as vehicles for students to express existing abilities or to learn a new form of art at the collegiate level (Tenhouse, 2018).

Other Activities

Most institutions offer a plethora of other activities that students may engage in. Honor societies give public recognition to students within an academic concentration who attain high academic achievement. Religious organizations provide fellowship and opportunities to explore one's faith and spiritual beliefs with others. Campus media organizations provide students with the opportunity to write or take photographs for campus use or DJ at a radio station or at campus events (Tenhouse, 2018).

Benefits of Extracurricular Activities

Getting involved on campus, whether it be by joining a group or participating in extracurricular activities, such as athletics, is one of the best ways to become connected, form a sense of belonging, develop and grow outside the classroom, and become engaged (Lau et al., 2013; Rhone, 2018). Research has shown that students, who engage in activities outside of the classroom, develop into well-rounded individuals (Lau et al., 2013; Tenhouse, 2018). Working with others ensures that students develop their social and interpersonal skills as well as their emotional and intellectual skills (Lau et al., 2013; Tenhouse, 2018).

Professional Skill Development

Extracurricular activities can provide students with professional skills that future employers will be seeking in potential employees (Mountain Heights Academy, 2018; Tenhouse, 2018). Leadership-oriented club, for example, help students learn the essential skills needed for management and delegation. In turn, athletic teams foster strong team-building skills, train students to pursue long-term goals, and teach students to maintain patience and build resilience (Mountain Heights Academy, 2018). Clubs and organizations, even those that appear to have little benefit other than having fun, not only serve as a learning experience, but connect students with similar interests and provide students with a well-rounded résumé for potential employers as well (Rhone, 2018).

Taking part in extracurricular activities allows students to learn negotiation and communication skills, how to manage conflict, and how to lead others (Zhang, 2016). Such attributes as good time management, thinking critically, and learning to listen to and respect diverse viewpoints are some of the offshoots of such participation. Students become more comfortable with their own leadership skills, especially as they relate to working with a variety of other individuals; these are incredibly valuable skills for life after college (Zhang, 2016). Tenhouse (2018) discovered that other attributes are gained; these include developing a stronger sense of an autonomous self and an appreciation for social diversity. Students also became more astute at understanding their own unique proclivities, assets, and career goals (Tenhouse, 2018).

Higher GPAs

Research shows that students who participate in extracurricular and cocurricular activities study more, have higher GPAs, and are more satisfied with their social lives (Rhone, 2018; Zhang, 2016). According to one student engagement study, the average college student participates in two campus activities with students from smaller colleges becoming involved in more organizations than their peers attending larger colleges and universities (Rhone, 2018). In addition, 25% of students reported an increase in their grades since joining a campus organization (Rhone, 2018).

School and Social Life Balance

While extracurricular activities go beyond supplementing education and imparting stronger professional skills by offering students the opportunity to spend time with other students that hold similar interests and meet friends from different social groups, students should take care to avoid participating in too many activities and carefully choose those that will benefit their circumstances and enhance their learning experiences (Mountain Heights Academy, 2018; Rhone, 2018; Tenhouse, 2018). Research has demonstrated that although 65% of students feel that participating in campus activities helps them balance their social and academic lives, 14% believe that these outside commitments caused their grades to drop (Rhone, 2018).

Time Management

Students that add more commitments, such as extracurricular activities, to their already laden down academic schedule believe that their time management skills actually improve (Mountain Heights Academy, 2018). Balancing two or more activities actually requires students to plan out time dedicated to each activity and makes them less likely to procrastinate during any downtime they may have (Mountain Heights Academy, 2018). Students have also found that non-academic related activities help them to refresh their mind and recharge after a day of rigorous schoolwork (Mountain Heights Academy, 2018).

Student Retention

Extracurricular activities build connected campuses, helping to form communities among students and boosting retention rates (Tenhouse, 2018; Zhang, 2016). Beyond the formal content of the extracurricular activity itself, these experiences help students build bonds with others, work towards common institutional goals, and strengthen attachment to the college and its mission (Tenhouse, 2018). Persistence to graduation, it has been found, is firmly rooted in feeling connected to others on campus, and these connections promote prosocial development as well as academic achievement (Zhang, 2016). Feeling that one matters, is cared about by others and has something to contribute to the life of the campus correlates positively with retention to graduation (Hsu, Acosta, & Hsu, 2013; Tenhouse, 2018).

Engaging Athletes

Athletic departments place a high value on community engagement as evidenced by their department websites, which often feature the school's mascot and athletes organizing charity events and programs on awareness (Heffernan, 2016). While these efforts are great for public relations, they do not necessarily meet the public purpose of higher education in preparing students for the duties of good citizenship (Heffernan, 2016). The charitable, apolitical, and needs-oriented approach taken by many college athletic departments are rarely transformative for students as they do not require student-athletes to build relationships within the community or reflect upon the structural forces which created the need in the first place (Heffernan, 2016).

Engaging student athletes becomes challenging and complex as, historically, athletic departments do not collaborate well with academic departments and do not envision themselves as part of school's teaching and learning agenda (Heffernan, 2016). Practically, student-athletes have very little time to engage in civic work and other extracurricular activities. Research has shown that athletes can spend anywhere from 35-50 hours per week participating in college sport-related activities, such as practice, competition, and travel, all while trying to juggle the responsibilities and demands that come with full academic loads, service expectations and jobs (Heffernan, 2016).

Participating in team sports requires students to work collectively toward a common goal, offers opportunities to hear different perspectives, and requires students to assume leadership, all experiences that will help them with the self-awareness and self-control skills that are necessary in today's democratic society (Heffernan, 2016). Athletics also affords students the opportunity to wrestle with concepts of justice, equity, diversity and duty while learning to temper and control impulsive behaviors and self-centered inclinations in the service of a larger, more collaborative goal (Heffernan, 2016).

Participation in athletics instills positive effects on a student's civic habits, skills, and dispositions. Students who are involved in sports are more likely than non-athletes to vote, volunteer, and follow the news (Heffernan, 2016). Belonging to and being a part of a team can also be a powerful and positive influence, particularly in demonstrating and reinforcing civic values, skills, dispositions, and knowledge (Heffernan, 2016).

The majority of athletes believe they have a responsibility to participate in service activities within their local community. Research has found that 87% of women athletes and 83% of men volunteer on an annual basis with at least 44% of men and women volunteering on a monthly basis (NCAA, 2014). Fifty percent of collegiate athletic departments have a community service requirement and this participation requirement enhances the likelihood that student-athletes will participate on a regular basis (NCAA, 2014). Athletes, and former athletes alike, report that volunteering with their team is a valuable experience and helped prepare them for life after college (NCAA, 2014).

Greek Life

Many college students see fraternities and sororities as vital to college life and student engagement. While there is widespread debate on the necessity and benefits of Greek life on campuses, sororities and fraternities can be a unique asset to a college campus and can serve as a premier leadership program (Nair & Chan-Frazier, 2017).

Leadership. Sororities and fraternities, as student-led organizations, aim to involve their members in campus-based and community service efforts. Each chapter provides leadership within its organization and its members can serve on committees or hold an appointed or elected position (Lucier, 2018a; The Quad, 2018; University of Wisconsin-Stevens Point, 2018). Students may also serve as a leader for the entire Greek community participating in the Inter-Greek Council (IGC) as well as serve on, and participate in, many other student organizations on their campus (Lucier, 2018a; University of Wisconsin-Stevens Point, 2018).

Scholarship. Students that participate in Greek life are expected to maintain not only the institution's academic standards but the IGC constitutional students as well and, as such, organizations offer a support system for students struggling with their academics (University of Wisconsin-Stevens Point, 2018). Greek life members can serve as a resource for students on professors and classes, can serve as an academic tutor, or just provide simple academic advice (Lucier, 2018a).

Community service & philanthropy. Many sororities and fraternities endeavor to instill a culture of service and philanthropy and recognize the most outstanding chapter's service achievements with a national award (The Quad, 2018). While involvement in philanthropic activities can vary from one organization and/or chapter to the next, most chapters provide students with the opportunity to become involved in a community service project (The Quad, 2018). Individual Greek life chapters, for example, may participate in service events, including volunteering, for a required number of hours or hosting an annual event to raise funds for a local community non-profit organization (Lucier, 2018a; University of Wisconsin-Stevens Point, 2018).

Support. The Greek community has historically been founded upon the ideas of sister/brotherhood and each chapter provides a sense of community and belonging, while still encouraging its members to become more culturally diverse (University of Wisconsin-Stevens Point, 2018). Through Greek organizations, students will also develop strong, personal friendships that can last a lifetime based on shared values and experiences (Lucier, 2018a).

These long-lasting relationships can also serve as networking opportunities and professional connections to members and former members well into the future (Lucier, 2018a; The Quad, 2018). Networks built through Greek organizations can be beneficial when students are looking for internships, employment, or recommendations and the connections between members can be valuable for landing interviews, listing references, or getting letters of recommendation (The Quad, 2018).

Final Thoughts

The majority of college students have their best learning experiences outside of the classroom through cocurricular and extracurricular activities. As such, today's colleges and universities have undertaken the educational mission of developing students as whole individuals and providing them with the opportunity to become involved in a vast array of diverse opportunities and activities which will not only complement the academic curriculum but augment the students' educational experience.

Participation in activities such as student government, athletics, professional organizations, multicultural and/or service related activities will help students attain higher grade point averages, develop better time management, develop professional and leadership skills, and retain students in school. For many students, participating in extracurricular activities they find interesting and compelling not only helps keep them motivated and engaged but also provides them with authentic, hands-on opportunities to hone their skills, put ideas into practice, and showcase their achievements.

Engaging students can be complex in that many students are limited in time and have outside obligations and responsibilities to meet. Engaging athletes is even more complex in that athletic departments do not have a history of collaborating with academic departments nor envision themselves as part of the school's academic agenda. Despite demanding practice and game schedules, most athletes believe they have a responsibility to participate in other extracurricular service activities within the colleges outside community and feel the valuable experience of doing so prepares them for life beyond college.

Greek organizations provide a parallel experience to that of participation in college sports for so many students. Becoming part of a community fills the need for connection, and most Greek houses involve a commitment to participate in service activities that benefit the college and community. Friendships built within these houses often last a lifetime.

Points to Remember

- *Those who are active in extracurricular activities have higher levels of engagement in and commitment to their institutions.*
- *Students who participate in diverse extracurricular activities develop across all domains—academic, social, personal.*
- *Students who participate in extracurricular activities and spend time with other students who share similar interests have been found to study more, have higher GPAs, and are more satisfied with their social lives.*
- *Students should be careful to not overcommit themselves and choose the right number of activities that will enhance their learning without incurring a detrimental effect on their academic success.*
- *As an extracurricular activity, athletics can provide students with unique opportunities to work collectively, hear different perspectives, and develop their self-awareness and self-control skills. Athletics also gives students the opportunity to explore concepts of justice, equity, and diversity in the service of a larger, more collaborative goal.*
- *Students who enter the Greek life, serve as mentors, tutors, and advisors to other students in need. These skills serve as building blocks for future jobs.*

Chapter Nine

Educational Equity: Promoting Access and Success for Diverse Students

Institutions of higher education are more commonly prioritizing access to high-impact practices that promote student success and retention. Although faculty members typically facilitate high-impact experiences within a student's academic discipline, academic advisors are uniquely positioned to also connect students to these experiences (Putnam & Rathburn, 2017). Given the focus on accountability on today's college campuses, it is critical for advisors to employ creative strategies that cultivate meaningful partnerships with faculty while maintaining a focus on student engagement, retention, success, and graduation (Association of American Colleges and Universities, 2018; Putnam & Rathburn, 2017).

Advisors have a responsibility to provide students with academic guidance, as well as to promote student engagement and "high-impact practices that provide the deep learning opportunities that characterize transformational education" (Association of American Colleges and Universities, 2018, n.p.). Although academic advisors are well-connected to their students and aware of their interests, they may lack the knowledge of high impact research projects and service-learning sites that will enhance student engagement in the classroom (Putnam & Rathburn, 2017).

Attracting A Diverse Student Body

Advisors, in collaboration with faculty members, may consider the development of an online application that gives students the opportunity to indicate their interest in a cocurricular experience and/or discipline-related activity. Applications should be designed to encourage students from underrepresented populations, such as first-generation and racial/ethnic minorities, and allow all students the opportunity to go through an application process and practice their professional skills, potentially making the exercise more meaningful (Putnam & Rathburn,

2017). As a result of the application process, some colleges have seen a ten-fold increase in undergraduate student involvement and a 30% increase in first-generation and racial/ethnic minority student participation (Putnam & Rathburn, 2017).

Research has demonstrated that high impact practices promote deep learning and are beneficial for college students from a variety of backgrounds and facilitate and increase rates of student engagement and retention (Association of American Colleges and Universities, 2018; Putnam & Rathburn, 2017).

First-Year Experiences

First-year seminars bring faculty and students together in small groups on a regular schedule and place a strong emphasis on critical inquiry, frequent writing, information literacy, collaborative learning, and other skills that develop students' intellectual and practical competencies (Association of American Colleges and Universities, 2018; Putnam & Rathburn, 2017).

Writing-Intensive Courses

These courses encourage and emphasize writing across the curriculum. Having students produce and revise "various forms of writing for different audiences in different disciplines" (Kuh, n.d, n.p.). Ensuring that all professors emphasize the same writing style and concepts leads to "parallel efforts in such areas as quantitative reasoning, oral communication, information literacy, and, ... ethical inquiry" (Kuh, n.d., n.p.).

Learning Communities

The integration of learning is explicitly linked to learning communities as instructors ask students questions that are meaningful and relevant to the real world (Kylte, 2004; Kuh, 2018). Students who participate in learning communities linked classes with other students and professors who share the same interests (Kuh, Kinzie, Buckley, Bridges, & Hayek, 2006).

Service Learning

Service learning has been demonstrated to be an effective strategy, especially for first-generation students. Learning in the field, in ways that are often hands-on and connect students with community members, suits the needs of so many students. Being able to compare and contrast textbook and classroom learning with real issues that communities face reinforces the content while encouraging students to see themselves as problem-solvers of real importance (Fong, 2014). In the best service learning courses, student will have the opportunity not only to apply reading to praxis but also to reflect upon their experiences in order to inform not only cognate knowledge but possible future career paths (New, 2016).

Portfolios

ePortfolios enable students to electronically collect their work over time, reflect upon their personal and academic growth; they are valuable artifacts that can demonstrate competency to faculty, advisors, or future employers. Because they are created over the various semesters, they can represent knowledge gleaned from sources both in and out of the classroom and students should be encouraged during their creation to make links between many diverse experiences they have had during enrollment, as all have played a part in learning (Association of American Colleges and Universities, 2018).

Senior/Capstone Experiences

Final learning experiences that culminate in reflection and demonstration of competence are popular on contemporary campuses. These represent the creation of new and synthesized knowledge and can be expressed through academic projects, demonstrations, exhibits, professional portfolios, or artistic performances (Association of American Colleges and Universities, 2018; Putnam & Rathburn, 2017).

Undergraduate Research

Being able to conduct original research with one's college professors is cited as a high-impact practice that has lasting effects on students' academic achievement, personal development, and overall satisfaction with their college experience as a whole (Putnam & Rathburn, 2017). Research projects, particularly those in field-based science disciplines, build students' skills in evaluating their field-based learning and transferring classroom learning to other situations; this consolidates deeper learning of concepts and is excellent career preparation (Association of American Colleges and Universities, 2018; Putnam & Rathburn, 2017). Conducting original research entails inquiry based on important questions of academic and societal importance, becoming a skilled observer, testing hypotheses, engaging in interviews, and using cutting-edge technologies (Association of American Colleges and Universities, 2018).

College Unbound

Adult learners and underrepresented populations would benefit most from community-based learning, capstone projects, and learning communities; yet, these high-impact educational practices are often not available to these students (Roy et al., 2017). It is essential that the 37 million United States adults between the ages of 25 and 64 who "attended a college without ever earning a degree or credential...[have] access to educational programs that have been intentionally designed to support their success" (Roy et al., 2017, n.p.).

College Unbound in Rhode Island is uniquely situated to do just that (College Unbound, n.d.a). Founded in 2009, this unique postsecondary institution is specifically designed for minority, underserved, and underrepresented adult students and offers a curriculum that only consists of high-impact practices (Roy et al., 2017). Integrative programs that include competency-based education, credit hours separate from seat time, prior learning assessments, and pedagogies that prepare students for careers provide students with an education that supports civic agency and enables students to be successful academically and in their real life (College Unbound, n.d.a; Roy et al., 2017).

College Unbound (n.d.a) reinvents higher education "using a model that is individualized, interest-based, project-driven, workplace-enhanced, cohort-supportive, flexible, supportive, and affordable" (College Unbound, 2017). Its responsive curriculum helps "students develop strong intellectual and practical skills along with a sense of civic professionalism and social responsibility" (Roy et al., 2017, n.p.).

Through the colleges work-related courses, adult learners are able to "make connections between their curricular and workplace experiences through multi-semester projects that feed their interests and goals while benefiting the organizations in which they work" (Roy et al., 2017, n.p.). Students identify their strengths and hone their academic skills while engaging in coursework that is designed specifically for them; thus, allowing the learner to complete tasks, and even their degree, while working (Roy et al., 2017).

Traditional colleges and universities may benefit from focusing on the learning outcomes set forth by College Unbound (n.d.b): (1) advocacy for self and others, (2) communication, (3) collaboration, (4) accountability, (5) reflection, (6) critical thinking, (7) intercultural engagement, (8) problem solving, (9) creativity, and (10) resiliency. As students achieve these outcomes, they will develop lifelong skills and "they become empowered leaders who are able to deal with diversity, complexity, and change" (Roy et al., 2017, n.p.).

Achieving Educational Equity and Engagement Through Technology

All students should have the opportunity to experience engaging and empowering learning that prepares them to be active, creative, knowledgeable, and ethical participants in a globally connected society. To be successful, students will need different pathways and opportunities to acquire expertise and form meaningful connections to peers and mentors (U.S. Department of Education, 2017). In the past, these paths and opportunities have been limited by the resources within a classroom's walls. With the advance of technology-enabled learning, students can now access experts not only in their own community but around the globe (U.S. Department of Education, 2017).

Technology can be transformative in the learning process by strengthening relationships between students and educators, creating new ways and means to create knowledge through collaboration, narrowing the gaps in equal access to technology, and individualizing learning to meet students' particular needs and interests (U.S. Department of Education, 2017; Young, Jean, & Quayson, 2017). Having a technology-enabled learning environment allows less experienced students to access and participate in specialized communities of practice and as they gain experience, move to more complex activities and deeper participation (U.S. Department of Education, 2017).

Technology has the possibility of being a leveling agent by giving the historically disadvantaged equal opportunities to access the same quality learning experiences that their more privileged classmates have had; these experiences include materials, individualized learning, career preparatory sites, and other forms of electronic expertise (U.S. Department of Education, 2017). Given that advances in technology can be coupled with the tenets of universal design, there are limitless opportunities for encouraging diverse learners to approach materials in multiple ways (CAST, 2018; Young, Jean, & Quayson, 2017). They also can use multiple means of expression to demonstrate what they have learned. Ranging from digital books and software, to text-to-speech features, the latest in technology creates ever-growing avenues to teaching, learning and assessment (CAST, 2018).

Student interest and motivation is likely piqued when modern technological tools can be implemented in lessons. Alternative formats not typically found within the classroom, including mobile devices, laptops, and networked systems, have great potential to increase contemporary students' engagement levels (CAST, 2018; U.S. Department of Education, 2017). Using alternative means of technology and available social media tools, educators are able to better personalize and customize environments that will align with the needs of each individual student and expand communication with mentors, peers, and colleagues (U.S. Department of Education, 2017).

Technology has the ability to capture students' attention by tapping into their interests and passions and help instructors align how students learn with what they learn (U.S. Department of Education, 2017). With technology, a student's learning experience can be his or her choice, making the experience more engaging, meaningful, and relevant; for example, students may choose from a variety options such as writing essays, producing media, building websites, and even collaborating with experts across the world (Southern Methodist University, n.d.).

The best learning takes place when it is situated in actual local and global problems and challenges; project-based learning and that which involves higher-order problem solving is most meaningful. Many different digital devices and resources permit demonstration of learning and competency in skills attainment in the contemporary classroom (CAST, 2018; U.S. Department of Education, 2017). Technology has the magical power to move learning outside of the walls of a classroom and into engaging settings such as museums, archeological sites, libraries, and even classrooms in other countries (U.S. Department of Education, 2017).

Access to technology, when equitable, can help close the digital divide and make transformative learning opportunities available to all learners; for example, a student with limited physical access to education can upskill by taking advantage of online programs to earn his or her degree and can accomplish his or her goals regardless of location (U.S. Department of Education, 2017).

Instructors, however, must recognize that there is still a disparity between students who use technology to create, design, build, explore, and collaborate and those who simply use technology to consume media passively (U.S. Department of Education, 2017). Merely having access to technology ensures nothing about the quality of a learner's engagement or the learning experience itself. A larger educational concern lies in the implementation of technology in meaningful learning; without intentionality in the manner in which technology is incorporated into contemporary curriculum, the digital divide could well increase even in the face of greater access to technology in our institutions (U.S. Department of Education, 2017).

Accessibility and Student Engagement in Online Courses

Online courses are unique and present their own challenges over the traditional classroom where professors see and interact with their students in real-time (Morgan, 2016). Without the face-to-face interaction and communication found in a traditional classroom, faculty cannot rely on the verbal cues and emotions to gauge their students' interest and motivation (Morgan, 2016).

Psychology tells us that students can be either intrinsically or extrinsically motivated and that students' motivation to learn in a particular setting can be influenced by his or her interest, perceived value of the task, self-confidence or esteem, and willingness to persist in the face of difficult challenges (Morgan, 2016). Intrinsically motivated students want to learn a skill or content for mastery or for their own fulfillment; they do not need external rewards to persist in difficult learning situations (Morgan, 2016). Those driven by external motivation are more likely to be motivated by grades or other external forms of reward (Morgan, 2016). In online courses, student motivation and engagement are essential, and faculty must find ways to boost both.

Rewarding the Successes of Students

All learners need rewards, and research has shown that praise can bolster both self-esteem and self-confidence, giving students encouragement to persist through difficult learning tasks (Morgan, 2016). Instructors should consider showing their students exceptional quality work from different learners to praise not only those students whose examples are shown, but to provide clear examples to motivate others to improve their own work (Morgan, 2016). If negative feedback is needed, instructors should be very specific in their feedback and avoid being upset and demeaning, even if unintentional (Morgan, 2016).

Faculty who offer extra credit built into their courses may also increase student motivation. Extra credit can be awarded for various accomplishments, such as timely submission of work over the semester or taking on additional assignments. Faculty who provide schedules with recommended due dates for assignments help their students stay on track for a timely finish but also allow for some flexibility when other life obligations arise that interfere with students' ability to meet those deadlines (Morgan, 2016).

Monitoring the Progress of Students

While some students are self-starters and self-motivated, other students may lack motivation and self-confidence when starting a new class or subject. To help motivate these students towards the course learning objectives and goals, instructors might build in blogs, collaborative group projects, discussion boards, and virtual office hours (Morgan, 2016). Faculty can load notes and examples to the online platform prior to starting the course, and class forums can be used to recap what has been covered in class, permitting students to review content and summarize learning to date (Morgan, 2016).

Creating an Accessible and Welcoming Student Environment

Instructors should strive to create an open and positive atmosphere that strengthens student motivation and sense of collaboration with the instructor. Because not all students share similar learning styles or derive their motivation from similar sources, instructors should include material, examples, and feedback relevant to students' academic concentration. It is imperative to incorporate multiple teaching styles and means of assessment in each course, as well, so that different learning styles and cultural styles are accommodated (Morgan, 2016).

It is important that students know that the instructor is not only an expert in his or her field, but a genuine human being who cares about his or her students and their futures (Morgan, 2016). Even though a course is held online, instructors can make online students an integral part of the learning community through personal introductions and ongoing exchanges (Morgan, 2016). Holding virtual office hours keeps students connected, motivated, and on task (Morgan, 2016). When an instructor is available at set times for discussions, questions, texting, email, or video conferences, students can receive immediate and timely feedback (Morgan, 2016).

Setting Attainable Course Goals

Students will succeed when their instructors foster a culture of success by requiring only meaningful assignments, gauging appropriate levels of class challenge, and setting realistic, but high expectations for all students (Morgan, 2016). A clear delineation of what is expected to earn particular grades and an instructor's willingness and readiness to help are all crucial to keeping students engaged and on the road to success (Morgan, 2016).

As success is defined differently for each student, instructors may also consider allowing students to set their own achievable goals for a course (Morgan, 2016). In all situations, one of the greatest gifts that instructors can bestow on their students is the support and encouragement to move students towards becoming more self-directed learners who can set their own goals and assess their own learning. Instructors who provide positive feedback early and often in their courses build students' self-belief and feelings of self-efficacy (Morgan, 2016).

Encouraging Participation in Curriculum Creation

When designing a course, student input can be invaluable. Incorporating topics that students recommend and want to learn about can make the class more enjoyable and enable students to more fully engage in the learning experience; their input, woven into course structure and required content, results in higher engagement (Morgan, 2016). One way to gain student input and insight involves using 'Great/Gripe' sheets, created to solicit student feedback on both assets and deficits in the course construction and content (Morgan, 2016).

In planning their courses, online instructors must be intentional in building engagement activities into the fabric of the course content (Morgan, 2016). But when they encounter learning situations in which students appear apathetic or are not meeting academic benchmarks, the best thing that instructors can do is poll their students for ways to improve the course experience. Research shows that students themselves are the key to countering student disengagement and that they are more powerful than any efforts to attach motivation directly (Morgan, 2016).

Supporting Student Engagement in Extracurricular Activities

Students face many decisions when in college and one of them is whether or not to participate in extracurricular activities or cocurricular activities. For some, the choice is already made for them as their decision is impacted by their backgrounds and support systems (Bye, 2017).

It is not only the support systems on campus that influence students' decisions, but the support they are provided emotionally and financially outside of the institution (Bye, 2017). Major financial barriers come with increasing student debt, next semester's tuition bill, today's grocery bill, and other family obligations and can prevent students from becoming involved in campus jobs, internships, study abroad options, and campus organizations (Bye, 2017).

Research has shown that students will have more meaningful relationships, develop transferable skills, and apply what they have learned in class to real-world situations and it is the responsibility of higher education professionals to account for the barriers to engagement and assist students in traveling a path to meaningful involvement (Bye, 2017).

To best support students, institutes of higher education should critically think about what their student engagement opportunities actually provide to students and ensure that student involvement has a direct benefit to the student (Bye, 2017). Faculty and staff should endeavor to share the vast amount of research showing the connection between involvement and post-graduate success and that the level of involvement can, and does, look different for each student (Bye, 2017).

Lower Fees

Although student affairs departments are constantly faced with budget cuts, institutions that offer fee-based programs should work to identify ways in which to cut or lower the student portion of the cost (Bye, 2017). Who is being excluded should always be considered when developing and offering off-campus programs, academic and cocurricular trips, and other fee-based opportunities (Wong, 2015). If fees cannot be cut or reduced, more doors can be opened for student participation by working collaboratively with other departments and/or researching what other funding opportunities may be available (Wong, 2015).

Funding Opportunities

Scholarship opportunities can be sponsored by colleges themselves or outside community organizations. Although students at the collegiate level are expected to research scholarships and additional funding opportunities on their own, it can be more meaningful when a staff or faculty member knows of a student's financial burden and can provide a recommendation that helps relieve his or her burden (Bye, 2017). Financial aid offices can be a great on-campus resource for students and staff and faculty should work collaboratively with them to make funding and scholarship information easily accessible to students (Bye, 2017).

Examples of Success

Sharing success stories of diverse people, particularly those from a variety of socioeconomic backgrounds and experiences, who have taken different paths to become engaged, can help affirm for students that there is not necessarily a "right way" to a successful educational career and life (Bye, 2017). It is imperative that students know there is more than one way to get where they want to go and sharing stories of a past student who worked two jobs, became president of a student organization, had an internship, and graduated summa cum laude is not the only story that can be told (Bye, 2017). To share a wide array of success stories and create more awareness that everyone can be involved, colleges may build mentorship programs that connect student with alumni who have had similar experiences (Bye, 2017).

Final Thoughts

Research has demonstrated that when colleges employ high impact practices, students from a variety of backgrounds can undergo a deeper sense and rates of student engagement and retention increase yet, they do not always reach the underrepresented students who can benefit the most from them. To be successful, all students should have engaging and empowering learning experiences that prepare them to be active and knowledgeable participants in society.

Not every student will take the same path to becoming engaged and gain the expertise needed to form meaningful connections with their peers and other adults. With today's advances in technology, students are able to use resources and experts located far from within the classroom walls. In addition, universal design methods and alternative formats provide multiple ways for students to engage in the classroom, more flexibility, and an increased support for learning. Alternative means of technology, including today's prevalent social media tools, allow educators to align the needs of individual students and customize learning experiences that will keep students engaged in relevant and meaningful academic experiences.

Points to Remember

- *Institutes of higher education that use interest-based, project-driven, workplace-enhanced curricula help students develop strong intellectual and practical skills, a sense of civic professionalism, and social responsibility. Students will develop lifelong learning competencies and become*

empowered leaders that can handle diversity, complexity, and change.
- *Technology can provide disadvantaged and underserved students with a greater equity of access to high-quality learning materials, expertise, and personalized learning by tapping into their interests and making their experience more engaging, meaningful, and relevant.*
- *There is a disparity between students who use technology to create, design, build, explore, and collaborate and those students who use technology to passively consume media. Access to technology alone does not guarantee access to engaging educational experiences or a quality education and without thoughtful intervention the digital use divide will continue to expand.*

Chapter Ten

Passion and Purpose: Engaged Students Need Engaged Faculty and Advisors

Engaged college students deserve equally engaged faculty members and advisors. In fact, the source of their engagement, as previous authors have noted, may well lie in the relationships and enthusiasm that faculty bring to their professional work. For students from marginalized groups and for those who need extra personal and academic support, faculty who demonstrate a true excitement for their work are the essential "hooks" for engaging these student populations fully.

Teaching and advising/mentoring are far more related to the helping professions than many might realize. College teaching is not practiced as though it were a technical science; instead, it is an art that also comprises a set of relational skills that other helping professionals, such as counselors, rely on. To view the state of contemporary college teaching and advising through this lens permits one to understand the myriad ways in which faculty and advisors fill roles far beyond those of conduits of knowledge and producers of scholarship. Faculty are asked to act "in loco parentis," which in contemporary times includes overseeing the human development of emerging adults and diverse others during a period in history when family and community instability are high and mental health issues rampant.

With campuses dealing with so many different student groups and their needs, the role of faculty has evolved into a multifaceted one, with far more attention to human dynamics, human development, health and wellbeing, student individuality, cultural awareness and mentorship. Each of these component pieces is extremely important to student engagement, but the combined effect of paying attention to each can be overwhelming. Add to that the continuing tsunami of institutional mandates and changes and the job threatens to feel nearly impossible at times. Yet, engaged students desperately need engaged faculty, both to bolster them during times of transition, challenge or self-doubt and to model the kind of passionate approach to knowledge and knowledge creation that results in the next generation of scholars and practitioners.

It may be hard for most individuals to think of the teaching profession—especially at the higher education level—as a highly stressful endeavor. Images of professors teaching light loads, taking frequent paid sabbaticals, and earning high salaries at prestigious universities mask the true nature of this work. College teaching, in fact, can be taxing, undermining the vitality and enthusiasm needed to challenge and support the diverse population of contemporary students entering higher education in this country.

Without a vibrant professoriate, all components of teaching, research, mentoring and scholarship are at risk. Minter (2009) succinctly addresses the issues of faculty resiliency by noting the high cost of its opposite "dysfunctional attributes, if gone unchecked and not discussed with the stress victim, can easily become chronic and negatively impact other faculty, staff, students, and program quality" (Minter, 2009, p. 1). He further takes academic culture to task for this, stating that "the irony is that university administrators frequently are reluctant to deal with the observable symptoms and behavioral issues associated with faculty burnout" (Minter, 2009, p. 1).

General Risks in the Helping Professions

Before one can consider the specific challenges of the professoriate, it is wise to review research and literature on the general stressors attending the helping professions as relational teaching and advising share many of the same attributes as other helping professions (Mullenback & Shovolt, 2001). These authors wrote of the numerous stressors that can affect a professional in education and the helping professions, diminishing his or her professional outcomes and personal satisfaction and affecting health. One primary stressor arises out of being challenged by job requirements for which the individual is not adequately trained and/or supported; this can frequently occur during times of change, reorganization, or shift in institutional priorities and can result in a diminished sense of self-esteem and efficacy (Mullenback & Shovolt, 2001).

Another common stressor involves not seeing progress or growth in the population of practice; for example, clients or students (Mullenback & Shovolt, 2001). The individual may feel stuck in a job, without mobility or avenues for advancement. Ruptures in peer relationships, as well as intrapersonal crises which impinge on employment, can cause additional distress in the workplace (Mullenback & Shovolt, 2001).

Compassion Fatigue

Figley (1995) wrote of the "costs of caring" in the professions mentioned above. Noting that those who worked with the traumatized often experienced secondary trauma themselves, he extended his observations to the realization that "the process of dispensing care can exhaust the care-giver" (p. 7). According to The American Institute of Stress (2018), compassion fatigue (also called vicarious traumatization) is "the emotional residue or strain of exposure to working with those suffering from the consequences of traumatic events" (n.p.).

The American Institute of Stress (2018) calls burnout "emotional exhaustion and withdrawal associated with increased workload and institutional stress, not trauma related" (n.p.) Figley (1995) noted that it is important to understand the causes of burnout, including secondary stress and concurred that burnout is emotional exhaustion that begins gradually and can take its toll in five different ways to include physical, emotional, behavioral, work-related (including work performance), and interpersonal. These can also manifest in "a reduced sense of personal accomplishment and discouragement as an employee" (Figley, 1995, p. 16).

Career Burnout

As Bartlett (1994) so astutely pointed out, "career burnout, in or outside of the academy, is fundamentally connected with the human need for meaning" (p. 3). Burnout is experienced as exhaustion in the emotional, mental and physical domains as a result of long-term involvement in work that is emotionally demanding. Pines and Aronson (1988) described three types of psychological characteristics of those individuals most at risk for career burnout, which Bartlett (1994) then elaborated on. These included the idealist: expects work to provide a sense of meaning; the overly caring: sees work as a calling; and the overachiever: views success as a measure of personal worth.

People fitting this profile are at high risk for burnout in a work environment that itself has specific characteristics to include a work environment that blocks or frustrates the individual's aspirations;; a work environment that takes more than it gives and provides few personal rewards in the face of stressors that cannot be avoided or changed, or the work load is either excessive or is not challenging (Bartlett, 1994). Rather than attempting to treat the faculty member for clinical depression resulting from work stressors, Bartlett (1994), suggested that depression and burnout were situationally-located, thus requiring changes in the work environment itself.

Challenges to Resiliency in Academia

According to Crosmer's (2009) doctoral research, faculty burnout has both internal and external sources. Studying 411 full-time professors nationwide, she discovered commonalities among the factors causing the professors' burnout (Crosmer, 2009). Chief among these were "lack of time, poorly prepared students, cumbersome bureaucratic rules, high self-expectations, unclear institutional expectations, and low salary. Research shows that the sources of stress have remained unchanged for 25 years" (June, 2010, p. 1). Crosmer (2009) also spoke about the prevalence of "presenteeism" in higher education, contrasting it with work-force absenteeism. In academia, "it means you're there at work, but mentally you're somewhere else. It's easy to hide burnout in education because every day you show up to work, you teach your classes, you advise your students" (June, 2010, p. 2).

The sad reality is that most seasoned faculty have done the work for so long that they essentially can coast on automatic pilot without being fully present in their work setting.

Crosmer (2009) also noted that tenure-track faculty were at the highest risk for emotional exhaustion, rating themselves towards the high end of a survey meant to study the high degree of burnout. Tenure-track faculty also had the most heightened levels of depersonalization, which indicates an impersonal feeling towards those one is supposed to be serving or instructing (Crosmer, 2009).

Reporting on the current climate on campus, Watts & Roberson (2011) reviewed scholarly literature and research on the deleterious effects of being a contemporary faculty member and noted that the job is no longer considered low-stress. Watts & Roberson (2011) include an analysis of 12 peer-reviewed, multi-national studies; findings included that burnout levels of higher education faculty were synonymous with those of health professionals and school teachers.

The authors tried to identify the major tipping points that deplete the emotional energies of faculty, resulting in what they termed depersonalization (Watts & Roberson, 2011). As depersonalization sets in, faculty become more negative towards others and feel less satisfied with their work environment. Among the findings are that younger faculty are at greater risk, as are women. Watts & Roberson (2011) postulate that newer faculty tend to have more contact with students, but it may also rely on veteran faculty's better-developed coping mechanisms. Women and men express burnout differently, with men having more depersonalization experiences and women more emotional exhaustion.

The researchers also found that having to be exposed to large numbers of students—as in large lecture courses—was related to burnout (Watts & Roberson, 2011). Sadly, it appears that the more engaged a faculty member is with students, the more likely s/he is to burn out. The very qualities that make for good advisors and mentors puts personnel at greater risk for the conditions mentioned previously.

Acedia

Bartlett (2014) is particularly interested in the concept of "acedia," which is experienced most acutely by faculty in the liberal arts, but it may be argued that this very experience is shared by all faculty members who teach in de-valued or under-valued disciplines. Acedia is "a form of psychological malnutrition in which an individual, or an entire people, has lost contact with the very realities that concern the classical liberal arts scholar" (Bartlett, 2014, p. 9).

Bartlett (2014) notes that today's college students, perhaps driven more than ever by the fragile economy, suffer acedia, "the barrier that stands between the man and woman who is a slave to the world of work and money, and higher values" (Bartlett, 2014, p. 10). This condition makes it difficult for faculty to inculcate the very values that drew them to their profession—learning for learning's sake, the desire to transmit beliefs and values that can positively transform society, and the beauty inherent in helping students find their true passions and callings in life; they must combat what Bartlett (2014) calls "vocationally compulsive tunnel vision" (p. 10).

As more and more underserved students gain college access, they tend to flood academic concentrations that they believe are pragmatic and will ensure employment and high wages; such choices include academic concentrations such as business, marketing, and accounting. The tragedy is that for many students, such career paths do not fit their talents, academic gifts, or interests.

The Career Life Cycle

Fessler and Christensen's (1992) early work on the career cycle of teaching professionals revealed that a career is comprised of distinct developmental stages, each of which has developmental tasks that must be accomplished if the individual is to experience job satisfaction. The authors define eight stages of career evolution to include pre-service, induction, competency building, enthusiastic and growing, career frustration, career stability, career wind down, and career exit (Fessler & Christensen, 1992). By way of example, a new college faculty member in the induction stage is challenged by a lack of experience and highly-developed skills which can make the newcomer feel as though s/he is treading water, just hoping to survive from day to day.

In a healthy academic environment, there would be mentors, departmental support, and lots of sharing by more veteran faculty who feel invested in the novice's success; in a dysfunctional setting, s/he may be isolated, receiving little support exit (Fessler & Christensen, 1992). Potentially, veteran faculty may even be threatened and overtly or covertly sabotage success. If left to flounder in a less-than-supportive setting, the new faculty member most certainly is at high risk for stress and burnout exit (Fessler & Christensen, 1992).

Fessler and Christensen's (1992) desired stage of attainment is enthusiastic and growing. In this stage, faculty have mastered the skills necessary to be highly proficient, thus freeing up time and energy for creativity, scholarship, and assignments that are personally meaningful, while also serving as excellent role models and/or mentors for other faculty members (Fessler & Christensen, 1992).

Skovholt & Trotter-Mathison (2016) articulated a developmental career life cycle, recognizing the tenuous balance/risk dilemma at each stage. While new faculty may need direct support and encouragement in a number of role-related tasks, more accomplished faculty would be at risk for boredom and burnout without meaningful ways to augment their earlier roles (Skovholt & Trotter-Mathison, 2016). Challenge and change are inherent in professional growth, and without them, faculty suffer personal and professional ennui.

The Family Life Cycle

Philipsen and Bostic (2010) conducted one of the most thorough and interesting studies on work-life balance in academia. Through interviews and examination of the policies of a number of diverse institutions of higher education, they discovered that the family life cycle could not be separated from the career life cycle of professors, and from their mental and physical health, job satisfaction, productivity, and longevity in the profession (Philipsen & Bostic, 2010). Life demands, such as birth, parenting, adoption, caring for an ill loved one, personal health crises, divorce, or tending to end-of-life issues all had a powerful impact on professional spheres (Philipsen & Bostic, 2010). How the higher education institution addressed these issues for each professor made all the difference in his/her ability to remain engaged and productive.

These findings are echoed in Bracken, Allen, and Dean's (2006) exploration of gendered perspectives in faculty roles and work lives. Although Austin (2006) notes that societal changes have influenced both male and female faculty members, when it comes to balancing work and family life, "aspects of faculty work still are not as promising for women as for men" (Austin, 2006, p. xii). Women are still more greatly hampered in promotion, tenure, pay equity, and scholarship opportunities due to pregnancy, birth, and care-giving to offspring and other family members, often including in-laws as well (Bracken et al., 2006). How well institutions did or did not do in creating workplace flexibility that allowed for integration of the two worlds was crucial in whether faculty, especially young faculty and those dealing with elders within the family or chronic or traumatic health crises, were able to remain engaged, productive, and committed to their institutions (Brackn et al., 2006).

A Narrative of Constraint

O'Meara, Terosky, and Neumann (2008) used the term 'narrative of constraint' to describe the commonly told story that emerged from their study of faculty and their work. The content of that narrative includes themes held in common among participants that express their emotions about the work that they do (O'Meara et al., 2008). Among these themes is "an overloaded plate and the lack of ability to manage it"—a factor that "pervades academic life" (O'Meara et al., 2008, p. 16). Faculty describe constraints inherent in "unfair tenure systems, work expectations, managerial reform, chilly climates, and lack of support and mentoring" (O'Meara et al., 2008, p. 16). There may be additional restraints relative to gender, race and ethnicity, and others that stem from working for under-resourced campuses or those striving to become prestigious.

The researchers found that those faculty who "reach beyond their socialization to take teaching seriously, engage with communities, and carry out disciplinary work [are far more the exception than the norm, citing that most faculty are just] treading water, given increasing pressures from technology, changing student demographics, entrepreneurism, and economic entrenchment" (O'Meara et al., 2008, p. 16). The saddest commentary on the state of the professoriate is that this study seems to confirm that teaching is indeed a lonely profession, with most faculty "lone rangers in often isolated departments or programs" (O'Meara et al., 2008, p. 17).

High Risk Teaching Assignments

Some teaching assignments, various authors argue, are inherently more stressful than others. McCammon (1999) wrote about the perils of teaching difficult material in the classroom - in this case, counseling psychology and women's studies. In discussing experiences with such subjects as trauma, abuse, rape, and the author noted that students may become re-traumatized through the teaching of these topics and that often they confront faculty with their emotions (including anger and sadness) that can cause faculty to experience vicarious traumatization (McCammon, 1999).

In some instances, McCammon's (1999) colleagues have stopped covering the emotionally-charged topics in class; others have initiated new strategies for introducing the material. While acknowledging the difficult act of navigating sensitive materials, McCammon (1999) stated that "the goal in tackling these topics is not to 'privilege the victimized,' or encourage them to 'wallow in scandal or melancholy'...but to increase students' knowledge and capacity for empathy" (p. 117).

Another potentially painful lesson can occur with faculty—particularly those who come from marginalized groups—as they may re-experience situations involving negative memories about when they themselves were students in the classroom (McCammon, 1999). All of the aforementioned situations put faculty at clear risk for work-engendered depression (Bartlett, 2014).

Conservation of Energy

Contemporary faculty studied by Neumann, Terosky, and Schell (2006) were caught in a web of often conflicting pulls on their time and energy "the need to learn pervades professors' work across the board: their teaching, research, service, and outreach" (p. 92). Simultaneously, in many instances, they are asked to 'do' while needing to learn how to do it. Faced with excessive professional demands, faculty often drown in the learning process. While love of their discipline or classroom teaching drew them to the field, they are not prepared for the additional demands of academic life, especially in an entrepreneurial era (Neumann et al., 2006).

> *Virtually all professors participating in our study struggled with this challenge: how to coordinate or balance the learning that drew them to lives of scholarly study and teaching in the first place, with new demands to learn new things, both related and unrelated to their scholarly interests* (Neumann et al., 2006, p. 92).

Without support and strategizing about how to best meet the myriad requirements of the professorial role, faculty deplete their energies and lose a sense of agency critical to job satisfaction and performance.

Public Perception of the Teaching Role

For many in the profession, public perception of their role jars sharply with their personal perception of its stresses. In 2013, the least stressful job was a college professor (Giang, 2013). The criteria used in the study included such elements as facing risk of harm on the job and physical labor (Giang, 2013). On its heels, the study was followed by a Forbes article (Adams, 2013), which opined the easy life of professors who are generally on vacation from mid-May to late August and enjoy "a month over Christmas and New Year's and another chunk of time in the spring" (Adams, 2013, n.p.). To make the job seem even less stressful, their classroom time is limited. Tenure-track professors are required to publish yearly; yet, even with that pressure, "working conditions tend to be cozy and civilized and there are minimal travel demands, except perhaps a non-mandatory conference or two" (Adams, 2013, n.p.). Such public attitudes reflect points made by Bartlett (2014) in his work on acedia.

Faculty on the Fringes

Much of the research on higher education faculty ignores realities of the contemporary campus. While it was once the norm that college professors were tenure-track, full-time employees, that hardly is the reality today; additionally, many are cyber-faculty, whose connection to the physical campus is limited, at best (Flaherty, 2017; Lewin, 2013). According to statistics from the American Association of University Professors 2015-17 survey, adjuncts comprise 40% of the contemporary college teaching force and teach half of the undergraduate courses offered at public institutions (Flaherty, 2017). The statistics further suggest reasons for adjunct faculty stress to include two-thirds receive course assignments two to three weeks before their courses begin; they have limited access to technology and privileges such as copying and curriculum guidelines; 94% receive no orientation; prep time is unpaid and they often provide their own money for materials and professional development; they most often do not get benefits, nor office space to meet with students; they teach more than double the number of classes each semester that tenured faculty do; and they find that adjunct work rarely is the path to a full-time position (Lewin, 2013). Eighty-nine percent of adjuncts teach at more than one school and they do not often have opportunities to interact with others in their profession (Birmingham, 2017).

Beating the Burnout

Hogan and McKnight (2007) have conducted one of the few studies of burnout status among higher education online faculty. After researching 76 online instructors at undergraduate institutions granting bachelors' degrees using a burnout inventory, it was concluded that the participants suffered an average level of emotional exhaustion; however, the participants experienced a high degree of depersonalization and low degrees of personal accomplishment. Male and female experiences on the emotional exhaustion scale were similar, but women experienced greater suffering in the two categories of depersonalization and personal satisfaction.

Faculty from Marginalized Populations

There may be greater pressures on those who are from underrepresented populations. As a junior faculty member explains

> *frankly because I was young and African American, I was not going to be a failure...I'm not going to be the loose chain or whatnot...When I first started here I had a lot of students come up to me and say 'wow, they finally did it (meaning, hired a person of color). And I just didn't want to be the person who...couldn't hack it* (Philipsen and Bostic, 2010, p. 108).

Institutionalized racism and the effects it had upon faculty of color was clearly delineated in research (Gold, 2008).

> *Often unaware of subtle forms of discrimination, white administrators are influenced by their personal ways of knowing that may be different from those of African American faculty. Consequently, stereotypical beliefs about African American faculty can proliferate. The inability of many white faculty to recognize their own racial privilege within a framework of widespread and systemic racism, often causes them to diminish research or dismiss publications that address topics involving related to race and ethnicity* (Gold, 2008, p. 55).

The author goes on to explain that

> *Faculty of color felt pressured between choosing "outsider allegiance" and "full insider status." They also expressed the need to work harder than others to justify their existence within the academy. As one of Gold's informants told her: "Well, I have done*

and continue to do what I need to do to get professional recognition. I decided a long time ago that I was going to do 3 or 4 or 6 or 10 times the number of publications that my colleagues have. But in general, to get the same recognition, African Americans have had to do more work in whatever field" (Gold, 2008, p. 103).

Gold (2008) also found that faculty of color confronted a feeling of impostership, based on the attitudes, comments and behaviors of majority colleagues that suggested there was

an old guard of the faculty who see the work of black scholars as illegitimate just because of who we are and what we did. To them, we aren't qualified or we are here for diversity sake or to make the department look good on brochures and in institutional research or for pictures (Gold, 2008, p. 106).

The experiences of gay, lesbian, transgender, and bisexual faculty essentially are all but absent from scholarly research and rarely discussed, while women still remain a population at risk.

Hult, Callister, and Sullivan (2005) describe the phenomenon as 'death by 1,000 paper cuts', whereby women are hurt by "ingrained assumptions, practices, and behaviors, often based on gendered stereotypes" (p. 52); for example, after women have children they are not serious about their careers. Female faculty in a 2010 qualitative study by Bingham & Nix found that women were more likely to report negative feelings about tenure selection, evaluations, and interactions with colleagues, as well as crushing workloads and work/family balance issues. The same group of women also reported that they spent more time than their male colleagues in preparation for class, committee work and advising and mentoring students, but were left out of opportunities for collaborative research and publication at the departmental level (Bingham & Nix, 2010).

O'Meara et al. (2008) review analyzed data on faculty perceptions of their work and the influence of those perceptions on career satisfaction and decision-making. It was found that perceptions have powerful impacts upon job satisfaction and exit from the higher education teaching profession. Female faculty members were less satisfied than their male counterparts when it came to advising, course load, and the quality of such things as job benefits, salary, and job security. Ethnic minority members, she discovered, were more likely to exit their institution and career than white counterparts.

Stress in Academic Advising

Huebner (2011) called academic advisors 'academic caregivers,' noting that they may experience compassion fatigue as the result of repeated work with traumatized students undergoing challenging or personally disruptive life events. Compassion fatigue among advisors reduces their capacity and interest in being empathetic to their advisees. When advising is a balanced process, it provides one of the greatest satisfactions of the role (compassion satisfaction) because the individual experiences positive aspects of being a helper.

In his study of academic advisors, Morrison (2013) found that those with fewer years of experience and/or higher advising loads experienced the greatest levels of compassion fatigue. Compassion satisfaction, Morrison (2013) found, does not have the power to mitigate compassion fatigue. Given how important advisors are in promoting student engagement, it is imperative that colleges and universities pay more attention to the risks for fatigue and the conditions that can enhance satisfaction so that advisors are role models who emanate engaged practice.

Schwartz (2018) wrote that the attitude that faculty and staff project towards students is related to whether students want to engage with them outside of the classroom or in other campus settings. Obviously, faculty and staff who are not able to project empathy and energy will not be magnets for students approaching them, both in class and outside and advisors who exude negative or flat affect will not have students lining up to visit them during advising sessions nor see them as role models for engaged living (Schwartz, 2018).

Hapes (2015) went so far as to develop an approached called PEACE (pause, evaluate priorities, assess process, create solutions, encouragement) because of the contributing factors to advisor burnout that need to be mitigated and countered. While most advisors are aware of the deleterious effects of stress on students' long-term health and wellbeing, they rarely deal with their own continuous stress (Hapes, 2015).

Defining Resiliency

Historically, researchers have studied resiliency to determine how individuals adapted to adversity. These studies focused on those who 'defied the odds' or who succeeded in life beyond the confines of their class, culture, or time in history. Reich, Zautra, & Hall (2010) defined resiliency as "an outcome of successful adaptation to adversity" (p. 4). They pose two fundamental questions that need to be raised when considering resiliency (1) How well do individuals recover from challenge?

and (2) To what level do people demonstrate the ability to move forward in the face of challenge? (Reich et al., 2010). Those who display resilient traits regain balance more quickly psychologically, physiologically and socially when faced with stress.

Garmezy and Rutter (1983) spoke to the 'competency indices' of resilient people using six attribute terms. Resilient individuals, according to these researchers, have an internal locus of control and self-esteem. They are competent in the three spheres of human life – those of work, play, and love (Garmezy & Rutter 1983). They are self-disciplined and set healthy expectations for themselves, but they are also humorous in how they approach challenges. Resilient individuals are good problem solvers, positive in their life outlook, and exhibit high level critical thinking skills (Garmezy & Rutter, 1983).

Reich et al. (2010) sees 'ego resiliency' as a stable, essential trait of resilient individuals; this trait manifests early—even in very young children, who are better protected from life stressors because of their abilities to seek and maintain positive relationships; maintain confidence even in the face of threats; and possess insight into situations and other humans that helps them navigate challenging situations.

Wolin and Wolin (2010) noted seven resiliencies; key among these were morality, personal independence or autonomy, and a sense of initiative. Maintaining these three key self- components allowed an individual to increase personal resiliency in the face of adversity. As found in other studies, humor, creativity, and insight boosted a resilient spirit, while having positive relationships empowered individuals and giving them guides or mentors fostered their development (Wolin & Wolin, 2010).

'Defiers of negative prediction' were the subject of Wang and Gordon's (1994) work; they coined this phrase to describe those who were able to maintain optimal well-being, often even thriving, under conditions that would have crushed others. One seminal element of their outlook was that change was not merely inevitable, it was desirable, positive, and rewarding (Wang & Gordon, 1994). The defiers held to a 'spirit life' or sense of something larger than the self when seeking life direction and they were motivated to fight life's injustices and indignities by what the authors called 'healthy anger.' Unlike anger that immobilizes or depresses, this righteous anger fueled their actions towards effecting change. Like most in resiliency studies, they benefited from mentors; even the presence of one other supportive individual seemed to make a substantial difference in their lives (Wang & Gordon, 1994).

Brooks and Goldstein (2004) described resilient people as "those who have a set of assumptions or attitudes about themselves that influence their behaviors and the skills they develop" (p. 3). Such individuals are in part temperamental (internal) and in part based on life experiences (external). Because of this interaction of internal and external factors, attitudes that affect resiliency are fluid and can be changed, thus supporting the idea that resiliency can be 'built' (Brooks & Goldstein, 2004).

The body of work on resilient individuals is remarkably consistent in its identification of the common traits or qualities they possess (Werner & Smith, 1982). In addition to qualities already mentioned, the resilient were able to hold onto an optimistic sense of the future, even when suffering personally; were proactive problem solvers who anticipated and planned for upcoming events; and were able hold onto their own roots and beliefs and separate from unhealthy individuals around them. Their highly-developed social skills permitted them to court others who served as polestars.

Resiliency in a Professional Setting

Henderson and Milstein (2003) were among the first to discuss how resiliency could be built into institutions—in their case, in K-12 schools. The resiliency wheel provided a visual representation of how institutions could be created in ways that bolstered faculty and student resiliency; this requires the simultaneous actions of building resiliency in the environment and mitigating risk factors (Henderson & Milstein, 2003). The six major factors in the wheel included providing opportunities to take part in meaningful activities within the institution, consistency in fair in policy implementation, teaching skills such as conflict resolution and cooperation, providing caring relationships, and setting high but realistic expectations for performance (Henderson & Milstein, 2003). It is not hard to see how these elements are equally essential in higher education institutions.

More recently, the notion of building resiliency has been explored in higher education; for example, Evans and Schubert-Irastorza (2010) gave a presentation at the International Society for Exploring Teaching and Learning on how to use self-reflection and analysis activities to identify and strengthen resiliency traits and skills among faculty and staff. At the same conference four years later, Schubert-Irastorza and Fabry (2014) lent practical strategies for improving job satisfaction among higher education faculty. They all drew from the same assessment tool for examining the eleven most frequently mentioned work-related dimensions that affect work satisfaction and level of worker engagement to include work content, autonomy, growth and development opportunities, financial rewards, communication, supervision, workload, promotion opportunities, work demands, co-worker relations, behaviors, and meaningfulness (perceptions of significance and value) of the work (van Saane, Sluiter, Verbeek, & Frings-Dresen, 2003).

Youssef and Luthans (2007) researched the use of aspects of positive organizational behavior to build resiliency in the workplace. This involved developing hope in the participants through having them set goals and 'stepping' sub goals, postulate realistic pathways emphasizing approaching desirable results rather than avoiding undesirable ones, and take part in contingency planning should future obstacles arise (Youssef & Luthans, 2007). Participants began to express an optimistic style, as they were able to see how to anticipate possible stressful events and plan proactively for dealing with them (Youssef & Luthans, 2007). The researchers also found that the activities built participants' recognition of their personal assets and how to use them; this promoted greater resiliency (Youssef & Luthans, 2007). Such assets included confidence, social supports, the knowledge that they had risk-management strategies, and a more internalized sense of control.

Strategies for Strength and Resiliency

There are two levels of intervention that can help educators maintain vitality throughout the career cycle; one occurs at the individual level and one takes place at the institutional.

Promoting Personal Resiliency

On the personal level, professors need to be dedicated to their own health and well- being. Writing about the resilient practitioner, Skovholt & Trotter-Mathison (2016) noted the factors that sustain a healthy sense of self. These included one set of factors that related to meaningful participation in the lives of other people, feeling successful in being able to help them, and the recognition that the act of teaching is a difficult endeavor (Skovholt & Trotter-Mathison, 2016).

Individuals who thrived in their work were able to keep a good sense of humor, creativity and playfulness, set good boundaries, sought out peer and mentor support, were able to differentiate between ideal and realistic goals, and were lifelong learners (Skovholt & Trotter-Mathison, 2016). Such professionals were able to thrive in their careers by being able to tolerate professional loss, ambiguity, and normative failure in their careers (Skovholt & Trotter-Mathison, 2016).

Young and Michael (2009), in their qualitative study of helping professionals, found that their participants offered similar advice for staying healthy within their professional roles. Those entering helping professions were cautioned to pay close attention to physical, mental and spiritual health needs; as one wrote, "find something that is relaxing to you and schedule that regularly" (Young & Michael, 2009, p. 303).

Humor was mentioned frequently, as it allowed the practitioners to diffuse tensions inherent in their work (Young & Michael, 2009). A "solid spiritual foundation is crucial in providing help and supporting a job that is often very lonely regardless of the number of people around you" (Young & Michael, 2009, p. 303). Devoting time to activities outside of the profession—such as hobbies, volunteer activities, and family traditions - is essential to good health.

The study revealed the importance of practitioners maintaining strong interpersonal connections at work as a buffering agent against workplace stress (Young & Michael, 2009). Relations such as critical friend groups, being a mentor or being mentored, and affinity groups that work on institutional issues around shared interests and needs are ways to build the buffer and break down the isolation of teaching (Young & Michael, 2009). Another strategy is to strive continuously for meaningful personal and professional growth; this necessitates continuous reflection on what drew the individual to the profession in the first place and what excites him or her in the current work. Such reflection can be both individual and shared in groups; under the best of circumstances, it is an integral part of professional evaluation, allowing a professor to "remind yourself of why you are in the profession" (Young & Michael, 2009, p. 304).

Young and Michael's (2009) participants identified a constant theme revealed in all of the aforementioned research that a work-life balance was mandatory to having a healthy practitioner. But keeping both worlds harmonious is not so simple to achieve. At the personal level, this means developing an ability to compartmentalize to the highest degree possible so that there are impermeable boundaries between the two. One veteran practitioner interviewed by Young & Michael (2009) suggested it was necessary to keep a "home is home, and work is work" attitude; and "put your all into each as passionately as possible" (p. 305).

Recognizing the humanness of individuals in the teaching profession, it is only natural that there will be failures; yet this is a building block to resiliency. So, too, is recognizing an individual's core principles and values and holding to them as tightly as possible as a moral compass in one's work is important to well-being. Schon (1987) described a practitioner's work as often being mired in "the swampy lowland"—a place where "messy, confusing problems defy technical solutions" (Schon, 1987, p. 4). This is where teaching frequently wallows, necessarily, and the moral compass can lead to technical solutions, then to ones that are consonant with personal beliefs about best practice (Schon, 1987).

Many times, it seems that practitioners strive for a sense of stability and stasis in their work; this is completely understandable in an era of constant external mandates, tidal waves of required change, and intense public scrutiny of education, focusing on accountability, cost analysis, and outcomes; however, resiliency requires change, adaptation, and the willingness to undergo transformation—even if at times it is risky, frightening, or involves loss and grief (Skovholt & Trotter-Mathison, 2016). The four strategies for creating practitioner energy, creativity, and novelty are changing the individuals' population of practice, professional methods, working tasks, and allocation of time and energy to certain aspects of a role (Skovholt & Trotter-Mathison, 2016).

Strategies for Promoting Faculty Resiliency

Across multiple scholarly sources, the common threads to the answer of how to promote faculty resiliency appear remarkably similar.

Create a Culture of True Colleagueship

O'Meara et al. (2008) see professional development activities as one means of fostering collegial relations. Many faculty enter the profession due to a passion of the subject of study and the desire to share their knowledge and passion for that subject. Yet, "ironically, professional development programs rarely capitalize on such interests and passions. Rather than faculty feeling that they need to hide the origins of their deepest conflicts and passions, faculty professional development could create programs that invite them in, for example, by framing their content so as to make room for autobiographical reflection" (O'Meara et al., 2008, p. 174).

Faculty should organize by affinity groups, rather than rank, department, discipline, career stage or other more artificial groupings, so that they can form "webs of community" to study and problem solve in relationships that are "interdisciplinary and disciplinary, among faculty and with practitioners and community members inside and outside the academy"

(O'Meara et al., 2008, p. 179). Such webs counteract loneliness and isolation.

Philipsen and Bostic (2010) found that faculty who were able to balance the demands of work and personal aspects of their lives described their institution as a family that worked collectively to create a supportive culture. While many institutions had 'paper policies' that allowed for workplace flexibility in times of need, the ones that in reality had created supportive work environments were extremely intentional in communicating their policies and helping individual faculty, from the time of hire, understand what policies were available to them and how to access them (Philipsen & Bostic, 2010). More than this, taking such an approach confirms the necessity of passion as a key link to professorial vitality.

A Corporate Approach to Health and Wellness Issues

Forward-thinking companies consider human resources matters through the lens of employee health and well-being, which translates into greater productivity, job satisfaction, and company loyalty; this perspective also reduces costs related to health care, absenteeism, and personnel turnover. Watts & Robertson (2011) found that the first step in mitigating burnout and creating a healthier professoriate was the clear understanding that unreasonable stress occurs when individuals do not have the skills necessary to process it. On the other hand, stress-reducing activities, counseling services, peer support and mentoring, and an array of therapies will contribute to high morale, improved health, and work longevity (Watts & Robertson, 2011).

Faculty themselves can be influential in promoting well-being by sharing their regenerative strategies with colleagues. O'Meara et al. (2008) heard their interviewees talking about "a wealth of coping strategies.... included are multitasking, exercise, enjoying the outdoors to 'get grounded,' and refueling through hobbies and personal pleasures. There is talk about spirituality and prayer as a way to refocus the mind on the purpose of the professional and the people who might benefit from one's work" (p. 104).

Inventorying Personal Assets and Building Resiliency

Youssef and Luthans (2007), offered concrete examples of how using positive psychology, resiliency theory, and specially-designed professional development activities in the workplace can build faculty resiliency. Even among the most highly-competent faculty, there is a need to become more resilient, especially in times when personal and/or professional pressures are high. This can be the stuff of powerful professional development, as well as ongoing evaluation and supervision. Frequently, faculty are adept at considering resiliency building measures among students—particularly those labeled at higher risk for failure—but fail to consider their own needs (Youssef & Luthans, 2007).

Engage Faculty in an Exploration of What Matters

Faculty perception of their roles has a direct connection to job satisfaction and career persistence; thus, it behooves administrators to explore what has meaning for individual faculty members and try, as best as possible, to locate opportunities for meaning making within the work role, service to the institution, scholarship, and community engagement. What has meaning is not necessarily a static thing; therefore, administrators and supervisors can help their faculty recognize their career stages and developmental needs as part of the evaluation process, annually, if not more frequently.

Using a schema such as the one developed by Fessler and Christensen (1992), administration can ask faculty to locate themselves within stages, noting the strengths and challenges that they face in any stage and identifying institutional resources that could help them thrive. The simple question of what an individual needs to attain or remain in the "enthusiastic and growing" stage can identify institutional supports that can boost well-being and performance among its faculty (Fessler & Christensen, 1992).

Developmental goal-setting can be woven into reviews at all levels, as well as professional development activities and reflection in settings such as critical friend groups. When supervisors notice individuals who are at risk by being overwhelmed, bored, or stagnant in their work setting, they must address those risks head on and attempt to help faculty find resources that can ameliorate their dilemmas; this is a matter that is both fiscal and ethical in nature (Fessler & Christensen, 1992).

Find Alternative Ways to Reward Service

If the academy is to retain those faculty whose primary motivation and job satisfaction are derived from teaching, mentoring, and service—not simply research, it needs to seek ways to elevate the status of and reward these aspects of the faculty role on par with research and grant funding endeavors. In actualizing such a cultural shift, faculty committees need to work with administrators to create both visible rewards and awards, as well as considering strategies such as a "point system" in which various campus and community activities receive variable point assignments when making decisions such as promotion and tenure (Tagg, 2012). Within alternative reward structures, "link faculty endowments to collaborative work instead of only to individual work. If all the significant rewards are accessible only to faculty acting as individuals in private, then collaborative work with other faculty will seem a loss rather than a gain" (Tagg, 2012, p. 8).

Such an approach helps to address equity issues, as women and many ethnic minorities are socialized towards group rather than individual achievement. When thinking of the degree of public attention brought to achievements in such areas as research and athletics, the hope is that institutions can bring equal visibility to other categories of achievement that are the lifeblood of the campus. O'Meara et al. (2008) ask critical questions in regard to faculty reward systems such that

> *instead of asking how rewards systems can create satisfied customers, we might perhaps elevate the question, pondering how reward systems aimed at recruiting, supporting, and retaining faculty promote that faculty's learning as well. What networks, opportunities or webs of support might colleagues and leaders create to engender faculty growth?* (p. 119).

Recognize the Implications of the Career and Family Life Cycle

Ignoring career and family life cycle issues can cost higher education by forcing individuals to choose their personal life over their profession. While it would be nice to assume that major strides have been made in addressing equity issues among underrepresented faculty, issues raised previously suggest that there still is a great deal of work to be done. Colleges and universities hoping to attract and retain high-caliber faculty from these groups must continue to make study, open discussion, and policy changes a part of their strategic planning to level the playing field and raise faculty morale, productivity and commitment at the institutional level.

Regarding the family life cycle and its interplay with professional practice, Philipsen and Bostic (2010) looked to exemplary institutions and found flexible pathways at every stage of faculty employment. These strategies involved such things as promotion and tenure extensions, job-sharing, scheduling classes with an eye towards the needs of dual-career couples as well as parents, creating cultures in which faculty took turns covering for others on leave, providing on-site childcare, and broadening disability, family leave, and medical coverage (Philipsen & Bostic, 2010).

Those strategies, clearly articulated to all faculty, that help them lead balanced lives were referred to as 'enablers;' and an institution that is rich in enablers does itself and its faculty a great service as "whatever success (faculty) have…does not emanate from a vacuum, nor is it attributable solely to individual strengths and attributes that they, personally, might possess" (Philipsen & Bostic, 2010, p. 109). There are four powerful misconceptions that need debunking. The first is the "traditional notion of a linear career trajectory," (Philipsen & Bostic, 2010, p. 123) given that careers can be both flexible and very individual in nature, yet still be productive for the faculty member and the institution.

The second is the misperception that child and family leave are "accommodations (thus potentially stigmatizing) rather than legitimate parts of a career trajectory" (Philipsen & Bostic, 2010, p. 124). They further encourage higher education institutions to challenge long-held beliefs that work-life balancing policies benefit only certain faculty, rather than all faculty, and that institutions themselves are not responsible for helping faculty find balance in their lives.

Continue to Openly Discuss Difficult Issues of Diversity

As O'Meara et al. (2008) astutely noted "the legacy of prior discriminatory practice is hard to eradicate; traces of its past exist, open at times, more quietly at others" (p. 118) and ignoring this prevents any real systemic change. Rather than using more formalized bureaucratic means to achieving this change, the authors suggest regular faculty gatherings, study groups, and community or town meetings to discuss workplace reform. More research that studies the experiences of marginalized groups—particularly using qualitative methods that allow people's stories to touch others—can also be a starting mark for institutional discussion and action.

> *Rather than aiming to stem the departure of pre-tenure women and faculty of color from tenure-track positions-for example, as a result of challenges in balancing work and family or because of the inability to spend time on meaningful community service that will count in tenure reviews-perhaps institutions, and especially their leaders, should look hard at campuses themselves, striving to turn their colleges and universities into 'hospitable academic homes'* (Philipsen & Bostic, 2010, p. 119).

Final Thoughts

Without a doubt, when it comes to student engagement on any post-secondary campus, faculty matters. As Umbach and Wawrzynski (2004) noted:

> *the "best" universities and colleges of the future will be those that demonstrate the most effective gains in learning and learning skills among their students. Our results suggest that faculty seeking to improve their teaching might hold higher expectations of their students. They also should consider including active and collaborative learning activities in their classroom instruction or emphasize higher-order cognitive activities such as the application of learning or synthesis of ideas. Interactions with students in and out of the classroom also can have a profound effect on student learning* (p. 20).

Yet, we must be vigilant in creating conditions for faculty that promote their own engagement, and those conditions include opportunities to interact with peers and students in and outside of the classroom in ways that bolster their resiliency. Faculty advisors and mentors need the same conditions.

Clearly, the academy needs to concern itself with the resiliency of all faculty and advisors that it employs. The costs of under-performing, stressed, or disengaged faculty and advisors go well beyond the classic human resources management measures (absenteeism, health costs, substance abuse, retention). Because each faculty member or advisor directly impacts so many others—students, colleagues, the community as a whole—the results of his or her performance are magnified exponentially.

There are multiple ways that colleges and universities can employ knowledge of resiliency theory and research to directly impact faculty and advisor well-being. This includes both minimizing risk factors in the professional and personal spheres, as well as boosting resiliency among faculty and their significant other; however, this takes forward-thinking leadership that sees the value of faculty engagement, vitality, and retention and is willing to spend resources to achieve these outcomes, knowing the payoff in long-term outcomes. This requires a trickledown effect as healthy leaders' model resiliency for their faculty and healthy faculty model resiliency for their students.

Points to Remember

- *Students cannot be engaged in their college experiences if they are surrounded by disengaged faculty and advisors.*
- *College teaching and advising in contemporary society share many similarities with other helping professions.*
- *Like counselors and other helping professionals, educators and advisors can experience either the joy of compassion satisfaction or the deleterious effects of compassion fatigue.*
- *College personnel from underrepresented groups may be at higher risk for fatigue and burnout if their unique status is not recognized and reinforced in an inclusive culture.*
- *All helping professionals run the risk of stress, burnout, and disengagement if they do not attend to their health and well-being on a continuous basis.*
- *Students will not desire engagement in and out of the classroom with personnel who appear disengaged, disinterested or not empathetic.*
- *Higher education institutions need to make an investment in building a culture that promotes faculty and staff resiliency and well-being so that they can be positive role models for students.*

References

Adams, S. (2013). The least stressful jobs of 2013. *Forbes*. Retrieved from https://www.forbes.com/sites/susanadams/2013/01/03/the-least-stressful-jobs-of-2013/#608c8c936e24

Ahlquist, J. (2014). *30 ideas for a digital-friendly new student orientation*. Retrieved from http://www.josieahlquist.com/2014/05/27/ideasfororientation/

Allegheny College. (2018). *Developing positive leadership skills*. Retrieved from https://sites.allegheny.edu/studentinvolvement/developing-positive-leadership-skills/

Archambault, K.L. (2015). Developing self-knowledge as a first step toward cultural competence. In P. Folsom, F. Yoder, & J.E. Joslin (Eds.), *The new advisor guidebook:*

Mastering the art of academic advising (2nd ed.), pp. 185-201. San Francisco, CA: Jossey-Bass.

Armstrong, P. & Stanton, K. (2017). *Rethinking expectations about assignments*. Retrieved from http://www.nea.org/home/34817.htm

Association of American Colleges and Universities. (2018). *High-impact educational practices.: A brief overview*. Retrieved from https://www.aacu.org/leap/hips

Astin, A.W. (1984). Student involvement: A developmental theory for higher education. *Journal of College Student Personnel, 25*(4), 297-308. https://eric.ed.gov/?id=EJ309521

Astin, A.W. (1999). Student involvement: A developmental theory for higher education. *Journal of College Student Development, 40*(5), 518-529. Retrieved from https://eric.ed.gov/?id=EJ614278

Austin, A.E. (2006). Forward. In S.J. Bracken, J.K. Allen, & D.R. Dean, *The balancing act: Gendered perspectives in faculty roles and work lives*, (pp. ix-xv). Sterling, VA: Stylus Publishing

Barkley, E.F. (2010). *Student engagement techniques: A handbook for college faculty*. New York, NY: John Wiley & Sons.

Bartlett, S. J. (1994). The psychology of faculty demoralization in the liberal arts: Burnout, acedia, and the disintegration of idealism. *New Ideas in Psychology, 12*(3), 277-289. DOI: 10.1016/0732-118X(94)90006-X

Bartlett, S.J. (2014). *Acedia: The etiology of work-engendered depression*. Retrieved from http://www.willamette.edu/~sbartlet/Documents/Bartlett_Acedia%20-%20The%20Etiology%20of%20Work-engendered%20Depression.pdf

Baxter Magolda, M.B. (2008). Three elements of self-authorship. *Journal of College Student Development, 49*(4), 269-284. Retrieved from https://eric.ed.gov/?id=EJ803067

Bean, J.P. (2005). Nine themes of college student retention. In A. Seidman (Ed.). *College student retention: Formula for student success,* (pp. 215-244). Westport, CT: American Council on Education/Praeger.

Bean, J.P., & Eaton, S.B. (2001). The psychology underlying successful retention practices. *Journal of College Student Retention, 37*(1), 73-89. DOI: 10.2190/6R55-4B30-28XG-L8U0

Bingham, T. & Nix, S.J. (2010). Women faculty in higher education: A case study on gender bias. *The Forum on Public Policy.* Retrieved from https://files.eric.ed.gov/fulltext/EJ903580.pdf

Birmingham, K. (2017). The great shame of our profession: How the humanities survive on exploitation. *The Chronicle of Higher Education.* Retrieved from https://www.chronicle.com/article/The-Great-Shame-of-Our/239148

Bloom, J.L., Hutson, B.L., & He, Y. (2008). *The appreciative advising revolution.* Champaign, IL: Stipes Publishing.

Blose, G. (1999). *Modeled retention and graduation rates.* DOI: 10.1002/he.10805

Boucher, J. (2014). *How UNH used social media to welcome new Wildcats during summer orientation & move-in weekend.* Retrieved from http://www.edsocialmedia.com/2014/09/how-unh-used-social-media-to-welcome-new-wildcats/

Bracken, S.J., Allen, J.K., & Dean, D.R. (2006). *The balancing act: Gendered perspectives in faculty roles and work lives.* Sterling, VA: Stylus Publishing

Brame, C. (2016). *Active learning.* Retrieved from https://cft.vanderbilt.edu/guides-sub-pages/active-learning/

Brame, C. (2018). *Just-in-Time Teaching (JiTT).* Retrieved from https://cft.vanderbilt.edu/guides-sub-pages/just-in-time-teaching-jitt/

Braxton, J.M., Milem, J.F., & Sullivan, A.S. (2000). The influence of active learning on the college departure process: Toward a revision of Tinto's theory. *The Journal of Higher Education,* 71(5), 569-590. DOI: 10.1080/00221546.2000.11778853

Bridgman, M., Shreve, J., White, L., Heaviside, M., Dunshee, L., & O'Loughlin-Brooks, J.L. (2018). *Encouraging civic engagement on college campuses through discussion boards.* Retrieved from https://www.mesacc.edu/community-civic-engagement/journals/encouraging-civic-engagement-college-campuses-through-discussion

Briggs, A. (2015). Ten ways to overcome barriers to student engagement online. Retrieved from https://onlinelearningconsortium.org/news_item/ten-ways-overcome-barriers

Briggs, S. (2014). *How to make learning relevant to your students (and why it's crucial to their success.* Retrieved from https://www.opencolleges.edu.au/informed/features/how-to-make-learning-relevant/

Brooks, R. & Goldstein, S. (2004). *The power of resilience: Achieving balance, confidence, and personal strength in your life.* New York, NY: McGraw-Hill.

Bruff, D. (2017). *Teaching with clickers.* Retrieved from http://www.nea.org/home/34690.htm

Bruni, F. (August 19, 2018). How to get the most out of college. *New York Times Sunday Review.* Retrieved from https://www.nytimes.com/2018/08/17/opinion/college-students.html

Burack, C., Lanspery, S., Shields, T.P., & Singleton, S. (2014). *Partnerships that promote success: Lessons and findings from the evaluation of the Jack Kent Cooke Foundation's community college transfer initiative.* Retrieved from https://www.jkcf.org/wp-content/uploads/2018/06/CCTI_Report_Final.pdf

Burke, M.G., Sauerheber, J.D., Hughey, A.W., & Laves, K. (2017). *Helping skills for working with college students: Applying counseling theory to student affairs practice.* New York, NY: Routledge.

Bye, R. (2017). *The accessibility of student engagement.* Retrieved from http://www.presence.io/blog/the-accessibility-of-student-engagement/

CAST. (2018). *About universal design for learning.* Retrieved from http://www.cast.org/our-work/about-udl.html#.W69yoWhKg2w

Carlile, J. (2016). *What is a student mentor's role in my student's experience?* Retrieved from https://newsletter.byu.edu/story/what-student-mentors-role-my-students-experience-0

Center for Engaged Learning. (2014). *Learning Communities.* Elon University. Retrieved from https://www.centerforengagedlearning.org/doing-engaged-learning/learning-communities/

Chickering, A.W. (1969). *Education and identity.* San Francisco, CA: Jossey-Bass.

Chickering, A.W., & Gamson, Z.F. (1987). *Seven principles for good practice in undergraduate education.* Retrieved from https://files.eric.ed.gov/fulltext/ED282491.pdf

Church, M. (2005). Integrative theory of academic advising: A proposition. *The Mentor.* Retrieved from https://dus.psu.edu/mentor/old/articles/050615mc.htm

Clayton, P.H., & Kniffin, L.E. (2017). *An introduction to service-learning and community engagement as co-inquiry.* Retrieved from https://www.centerforengagedlearning.org/an-introduction-to-service-learning-and-community-engagement-as-co-inquiry/

Coles, A, (2015). *Reducing summer melt: Helping 12th graders successfully transition to college.* Retrieved from https://ccrscenter.org/blog/reducing-summer-melt-helping-12th-graders-successfully-transition-college

College Unbound. (n.d.a). *History.* Retrieved from https://www.collegeunbound.org/apps/pages/history

College Unbound. (n.d.b). *Competencies.* Retrieved from https://www.collegeunbound.org/apps/pages/competencies

College Unbound. 2017. *Mission.* Retrieved from http://www.collegeunbound.org/apps/pages/mission.

Cook, S. (2001). A chronology of academic advising in America. *The Mentor.* Retrieved from https://dus.psu.edu/mentor/old/articles/011015sc.htm

Cook, S. (2009). Important events in the development of academic advising. *NACADA Journal, 29*(2), 18-40. DOI: 10.12930/0271-9517-29.2.18

Creamer, D.G., & Creamer, E.G. (1994). Practicing developmental advising: Theoretical contexts and functional applications. *NACADA Journal, 14*(2), 17-24. DIO: 10.12930/0271.-9517-14-2.17

Crosmer, J.L. (2009). *Professional burnout among U.S. full-time university faculty: Implications for worksite health promotion.* [Doctoral dissertation]. Texas Woman's University.

Csikszentmihalyi, M. (1990). *Flow: The Psychology of Optimal Experience.* New York, NY: Harper & Row

Damminger, J., & Rakes, M. (2017). The role of the academic advisor in the first year. In J.R. Fox & H.E. Martin (Eds.). *Academic Advising and the First College Year,* (pp.19-24). Sterling, VA: Stylus Publishing

Davis, B.G. (2009). *Tools for teaching* (2nd ed.). New York, NY: Jossey-Bass.

Davis, J. (2010). *The first-generation student experience: Implications for campus practice, and strategies for improving persistence and success.* Sterling, VA: Stylus Publishing.

Drake, J.K., Jordan, P., & Miller, M.A. (2013). *Academic advising approaches: Strategies that teach students to make the most of college.* San Francisco, CA: Jossey-Bass.

Delaney, C.M., Edwards, I., Jensen, G.M. & Skinner, E. (2010). Closing the gap between ethics knowledge and practice through active engagement: An applied model of physical therapy ethics. *Physical Therapy, 90*(7), 1068-1078. DOI: 10.2522/ptj.20090379.

Drumgoole, Jr., J. (2018). The art of conflict resolution among leaders. *Forbes.* Retrieved from https://www.forbes.com/sites/forbeshumanresourcescouncil/2018/03/22/the-art-of-conflict-resolution-among-leadership/#6dc9e70e261b

DuBrin, A.J. (2016). *Leadership: Research findings, practice, and skills* (8th ed.). Boston, MA: Cengage

Earl, W.R. (1987). Intrusive advising of freshmen in academic difficulty. *NACADA Journal,* 8, 27-33. DOI: 10.12930/0271-9517-8.2.27

Eiser, A. (2011). The crisis on campus. *The American Psychological Association, 42*(8), 18. Retrieved from https://www.apa.org/monitor/2011/09/crisis-campus.aspx

Emmanuel College. (2018). *Tips for new student success.* Retrieved from https://www.emmanuel.edu/student-life/new-student-engagement-and-transition/tips-for-success.html

Engle, J. & Tinto, V. (2008). *Moving beyond access: College success for low-income, first-generation.* Retrieved from https://files.eric.ed.gov/fulltext/ED504448.pdf

Evans, S. & Schubert-Irastorza, C. (2010). Bouncing back from professional setbacks: Resiliency in higher education. In S.E. Copeland, *The 40th Annual Conference of The International Society for Exploring Teaching &*

Learning Proceedings, (pp. 80-82). Retrieved from http://citeseerx.ist.psu.edu/viewdoc/download?rep=rep1&type=pdf&doi=10.1.1.189.4138

Ferlazzo, L. (2011, May). Involvement or engagement? *Educational Leadership, 68*(8), 10-14. Retrieved from http://www.ascd.org/publications/educational-leadership/may11/vol68/num08/Involvement-or-Engagement%C2%A2.aspx

Ferlazzo, L. (2017). Student engagement: Key to personalized learning. *Educational Leadership, 74*(6), 28-33. Retrieved from http://www.ascd.org/publications/educational-leadership/mar17/vol74/num06/Student-Engagement@-Key-to-Personalized-Learning.aspx

Fessler, R. & Christensen, J.C. (1992). *The teacher career cycle: Understanding and guiding the professional development of teachers.* Boston, MA: Allyn and Bacon.

Figley, C. R. (1995). Compassion Fatigue: Toward a New Understanding of the Costs of Caring. In B. H. Stamm (Ed.), *Secondary Traumatic Stress: Self-Care Issues for Clinicians, Researchers, and Educators,* (pp. 3-28). Lutherville, MD: Sidran Press.

Finn, J.D., & Zimmer, K.A. (2013). Student engagement: What is it and why does it matter? In S.L. Christenson, A.L. Reschly, & C. Wylie (eds). *Handbook of Research on Student Engagement,* (pp. 97-132). New York, NY: Springer.

Flaherty, C. (2017). GAO report on non-tenure-track faculty. *Inside Higher Ed.* Retrieved from https://www.insidehighered.com/quicktakes/2017/11/21/gao-report-non-tenure-track-faculty

Fleming, J.H., Coffman, C. and Harter, J.K. (2006). Manage your human sigma. *IEEE Engineering Management Review, 34*(1), 52-59. Retrieved from https://www.researchgate.net/profile/James_Harter/publication/7715816_Manage_your_Human_Sigma/links/53e39af10cf2fb74870daafb/Manage-your-Human-Sigma.pdf

Fong, B. (2014). *Civic engagement is an essential element of a college education.* Retrieved from https://www.huffingtonpost.com/bobby-fong/civic-engagement-is-an-es_b_4962740.html

Fredshaw, P. (2016). *Why it is so important to develop leadership skills in college.* Retrieved from https://yourstory.com/mystory/3958df0bb7-why-it-is-so-important-to-develop-leadership-skills-in-college

Fuchs, S.J., Cannella, L.G., Pisano, S. (2014). College and community partnerships: Extending the benefits of therapeutic recreation to veterans. *Journal of Leisure Studies and Recreation Education, 29*(2), 10-24. Retrieved from https://eric.ed.gov/?id=EJ1035005

Galindo, J.H. (2018). *Classroom assessment, reflection & feedback.* Retrieved from https://ablconnect.harvard.edu/assessment-reflection-feedback

Garmezy, N. & Rutter, M. (1983). *Stress, coping, and development in children.* Baltimore, MD: Johns Hopkins University Press.

Georgia Tech. (2018). *Center for Student Engagement.* Retrieved from http://engage.gatech.edu/

Giang, V. (2013). *The 10 least stressful jobs of 2013.* Retrieved from https://www.businessinsider.com/the-10-least-stressful-jobs-in-2013-2013-1#1-university-professor-10

Gleeson, B. (2017). How values-based leadership transforms organizational culture. *Forbes.* Retrieved from https://www.forbes.com/sites/brentgleeson/2017/03/10/how-values-based-leadership-transforms-organizational-cultures/#1dae8de31fbd

Glennen, R.E. (1975). Intrusive college counseling. *College Student Journal,* 9(1), 2-4. Retrieved from https://eric.ed.gov/?id=EJ120693

Gold, R.S. (2008). *Outsiders within: African American professors and their experiences at predominantly white universities: A narrative interview study.* Unpublished doctoral dissertation. University of North Carolina, Chapel Hill.

Gordon, V.N., Levinson, J., & Kirkner, T. (2018). *Academic advising in the first year of college.* Sterling, VA: Stylus Publishing

Great Value Colleges. (2018). *Are extracurricular activities in college important?* Retrieved from https://www.greatvaluecolleges.net/faq/are-extracurricular-activities-in-college-important/

Griswold, A. (2013). 4 problem-solving tactics of great leaders. *Business Insider.* Retrieved from https://www.businessinsider.com/problem-solving-tactics-of-great-leaders-2013-11

Grites, T.J. (1979). Academic Advising: Getting Us Through the Eighties. *AAHE-ERIC/Higher Education Research Reports, No. 7.* Retrieved from https://files.eric.ed.gov/fulltext/ED178023.pdf

Grites, T.J. (2013). Developmental academic advising. In J.K. Drake, P. Jordan, & M.A. Miller. *Academic advising approaches: Strategies that teach students to make the most of college,* (pp. 45-60). San Francisco, CA: Jossey-Bass.

Habley, W.R., Bloom, J.L., & Robbins, S. (2012). *Increasing persistence.* Jossey-Bass.

Hapes, R. (2015). *The PEACE approach for balance and stress management.* Retrieved from https://www.nacada.ksu.edu/Resources/Academic-Advising-Today/View-Articles/The-PEACE-Approach-for-Balance-and-Stress-Management.aspx

Harper, R., & Peterson, M. (2005). *Mental health issues and college students: What advisors can do.* Retrieved from http://www.nacada.ksu.edu/Resources/Clearinghouse/View-Articles/Mental-health-issues-in-advising.aspx

Heffernan, K. (2016). *Engaging the student-athlete identity.* Retrieved from https://compact.org/engaging-the-student-athlete-identity/

Heiberger, G. and Junco, R. (2017). Meet your students where they are: Social media. *NEA Higher Education Advocate.* Retrieved from http://www.nea.org/assets/docs/HE/1109Advocate_pg06-09.pdf

Henderson, N., & Milstein, M. (2003). *Resiliency in schools: Making it happen for students and educators.* Thousand Oaks, CA: Corwin Press.

Hibel, A. & Hernandez, C.L. (2018). *New student programs: A look inside orientation, transition and retention programs.* Retrieved from https://www.higheredjobs.com/HigherEdCareers/interviews.cfm?ID=402

Hogan, R.L., & McKnight, M.A. Exploring burnout among university online instructors: An initial investigation. *The internet and higher education* 10 (2007) 117-124.

Holder, C.S. (2013). Academic advising in a multicultural world. *The Mentor: An Academic Advising Journal.* Retrieved from https://dus.psu.edu/mentor/2013/09/academic-advising-multicultural-world/

Hsieh, P. Sullivan, J.R., & Guerra, N.S. (2007). A closer look at college students: Self-efficacy and goal orientation. *Journal of Advanced Academics, 18*(3), 454-476. DOI:10.4219/jaa-2007-500

Howard-Hamilton, M. (2002). Programming for multicultural competencies. *New Directions for Student Services, 2000*(90), 67-78. DOI: 10.1002/ss.9006

Huber, J.A. & Miller, M.A. (2013). Implications for advisor job responsibilities at 2- and 4-year institutions. *NACADA: Clearinghouse.* Retrieved from https://www.nacada.ksu.edu/Resources/Clearinghouse/View-Articles/Advisor-Job-Responsibilities.aspx

Huebner, C. (2011). Coping with advisor burnout. Retrieved https://www.nacada.ksu.edu/Resources/Clearinghouse/View-Articles/Advisor-Burnout.aspx

Hughey, J., & Pettay, R. (2013). Motivational interviewing: Helping advisors initiate change in student behaviors. In Drake, J.K., Jordan, P., & Miller, M.A. (Eds.). *Academic Advising Approaches: Strategies that Teach Students to Make the Most of College,* (pp.67-82). San Francisco, CA: Jossey-Bass.

Hult, C., Callister, R., & Sullivan, K. (2005). Is there global warming toward women in academia. *Liberal Education, 91,* 50-56. Retrieved from https://www.researchgate.net/publication/44019006_Is_There_a_Global_Warming_Toward_Women_in_Academia

Hyun, J.K., Quinn, B.C., Madon, T., & Lustig, S. (2006). Graduate student mental health: Needs assessment and utilization of counseling services. *Journal of College Student Development, 47*(3), 248-266. Retrieved from https://eric.ed.gov/?id=EJ743920

Johnson, M.L. (2017). Engaging first-year students in academic planning. In J.R. Fox & H.E. Martin (Eds.). (2017). *Academic Advising and the First College Year,* (pp.151-164). Sterling, VA: Stylus Publishing

June, A.W. (2010). *Faculty burnout has both external and internal sources.* Retrieved from http://chronicle.com/article/Faculty-Burnout-Has-Both/65843/

Kadison, R., & DiGermonimo, T.F. (2004). *College of the overwhelmed: The campus mental health crisis and what to do about it.* San Francisco, CA: Jossey-Bass.

Kegan, R. (1994). *In over our heads: The mental demands of modern life.* Cambridge, MA: Harvard University Press.

Kitchener, K.S. (2000). *Foundations of ethical practice, research, and teaching in psychology.* Mahwah, NJ: Lawrence Erlbaum Associates.

Kniffin, L.E. and Clayton, P.H. (2017). *Why service-learning and community engagement.* Retrieved from https://www.centerforengagedlearning.org/why-service-learning-and-community-engagement/

Kuh, G.D. (n.d.). *Excerpt from high-impact educational practices: What they are, who has access to them, and why they matter.* Retrieved from https://secure.aacu.org/AACU/PubExcerpts/HIGHIMP.html

Kuh, G.D. (2006). *Thinking deeply about academic advising and student engagement.* Retrieved from www.nacada.ksu.edu/Resources/Academic-Advising-Today/View-Articles/Thinking-DEEPly-about-Academic-Advising-and-Student-Engagement.aspx

Kuh, G.D. (2018). What student engagement data tell us about college readiness. *peerReview, 9*(1). Retrieved from https://www.aacu.org/publications-research/periodicals/what-student-engagement-data-tell-us-about-college-readiness

Kuh, G.D., Kinzie, J., Buckley, J.A., Bridges, B.K., & Hayek, J.C. (2006). What matters to student success: A review of the literature. Retrieved from https://nces.ed.gov/npec/pdf/kuh_team_report.pdf

Kuh, G.D., Kinzie, J., Schuh, J.H. & Whitt, E. (2005a). Never let it rest: Lessons about student success from high-performing colleges and universities. *Change: The Magazine of Higher Learning, 37*(4), pp. 44–51. DOI: 10.3200/CHNG.37.4.44-51

Kuh, G.D., Kinzie, J., Schuh, J.H., & Whitt, E. (2005b). *Student success in college: Creating conditions that matter.* San Francisco, CA: Jossey-Bass.

Kuh, G.D., Schuh, J.H., Whitt, E.J., Andreas, R.E., Lyons, J.W., Strange, C.C., Krehbiel, L.E. & MacKay, K.A. (1991). *Involving Colleges: Successful approaches to fostering student learning and development outside the classroom.* San Francisco: Jossey-Bass.

Kuhtmann, M.S. (2005). Socratic self-examination and its application to academic advising. *NACADA Journal, 25*(2), 37-48. DOI: 10.12930/0271-9517.25.2.36

Kytle, J. (2004). *To want to learn: Insights and provocations for engaged learning* (2nd ed.). New York, NY: Palgrave Macmillan.

LaGier, M. (2018). Using assignment choice to promote course relevancy. *Faculty Focus.* Retrieved from https://www.facultyfocus.com/articles/effective-teaching-strategies/using-assignment-choice-to-promote-course-relevancy/

Lang, J.M. (2017). Small teaching: Lessons for faculty from the science of learning. *NEA Higher Education Advocate.* Retrieved from http://www.nea.org/assets/docs/1609Advocate_ThrivingFinal.pdf

Lau, H.H., Hsu, H.Y., Acosta, S. & Hsu, T.L. (2013). Impact of participation in extra-curricular activities during college on graduate employability: An empirical study of graduates of Taiwanese business schools. *Educational Studies, 40*(1), 26-47. DOI: 10.1080/03055698.2013.830244

Lewin, T. (2013). Gap widens for faculty at colleges, report finds. *The New York Times*. Retrieved from https://www.nytimes.com/2013/04/08/education/gap-in-university-faculty-pay-continues-to-grow-report-finds.html?_r=3&

Loria, R. (2018). A how-to guide for building school-community partnerships. *Education Week*. Retrieved from https://www.edweek.org/ew/articles/2018/03/23/a-how-to-guide-for-building-school-community-partnerships.html

Lucier, K.L. (2018a). *The benefits of going Greek in college.* Retrieved from https://www.thoughtco.com/benefits-of-going-greek-in-college-793356

Lucier, K.L. (2018b). *Opportunities for leadership in college.* Retrieved from https://www.thoughtco.com/opportunities-for-leadership-in-college-793360

Lutes, B. (2016). *Tools to facilitate in-class polling.* Retrieved from http://teachingcenter.wustl.edu/2016/09/tools-to-facilitate-in-class-polling/

MDRC. (2012). What have we learned about learning communities at community colleges? Retrieved from https://www.mdrc.org/publication/what-have-we-learned-about-learning-communities-community-colleges

Mangan, K. (2018). These 2-year and 4-year college partnerships keep students from falling through the cracks. *The Chronicle of Higher Education.* Retrieved from https://www.chronicle.com/article/These-2-Year4-Year/243283

Mansfield University. (2012). *Twelve best practices for student engagement and retention.* Retrieved https://www.mansfield.edu/academic-affairs/upload/Twelve-Best-Practices-for-Student-Engagement-and-Retention-2012.pdf

Maslow, A. H. (1954). *Motivation and personality.* New York, NY: Harper and Row.

Maslow, A.H. (2013). *A theory of human motivation.* Seaside, OR: Rough Draft Printing

McCammon, S.L. (1999). Painful Pedagogy: Teaching about trauma in academic and training settings. In B.H. Stamm (ed), *Secondary traumatic stress: Self-care issues for clinicians, researchers, and educators.* Lutherville: MD: Sidran Press

Merriam-Webster. (2018). Captivate. Retrieved from https://www.dictionary.com/browse/captivate

Meyers, S. (2014). Three strategies for creating meaningful learning experiences. *Faculty Focus.* Retrieved from https://www.facultyfocus.com/articles/effective-teaching-strategies/three-strategies-creating-meaningful-learning-experiences/

Miars, L. (2017). *The evolution of academic advising – and what comes next.* Retrieved from https://www.eab.com/blogs/student-success-insights/2017/04/the-evolution-of-academic-advising-and-what-comes-next

Michael, C.N., & Wilkins, V. (2014). *'She threw me a lifeline': Meaningful mentoring that retains graduate students.* CAEL National Conference, Chicago, IL.

Miller, K. (2018). *Can residential colleges and living learning communities enhance your college experience?* Retrieved from https://www.scoir.com/blog/residential-colleges-and-living-learning-communities-better-college-housing-options

Miller, W.R., & Rollnick, S. (2012). *Motivational interviewing.* The Guilford Press.

Millis, B.J. (2010). *Cooperative learning in higher education: Across disciplines, across the academy.* Sterling, VA: Stylus Publishing

Minter, R.L. (2009). Faculty burnout. *Contemporary issues in education research-Second Quarter 2009.* Volume 2, number 2. 1-8.

Morgan, B.M. (2016). *Student engagement: 5 strategies to motivate the online learner.* Retrieved from https://blog.blackboard.com/student-engagement-strategies-motivate-online-learner/

Morrison, J.D. (2013). *Improving compassion satisfaction and understanding compassion fatigue among academic advisors.* Retrieved from https://emas.illinoisstate.edu/downloads/aaac/CF-CS%20Illinois%20State%20University%202013.pdf

Mountain Heights Academy. (2018). *Why extracurricular activities are so important.* Retrieved from https://www.mountainheightsacademy.org/why-extracurricular-activities-are-so-important/

National Academic Advising Association (NACADA). (2017). *NACADA academic advising core competencies model.* Retrieved from https://www.nacada.ksu.edu/Resources/Pillars/CoreCompetencies.aspx

NCAA. (2014). *Playing it forward: Commitment to service among student-athletes.* Retrieved from http://www.ncaa.org/about/resources/research/playing-it-forward-commitment-service-among-student-athletes

NHIAA Life of an Athlete. (2018). *Leadership.* Retrieved from http://loanh.org/for-student-athletes/leadership/

Nan, A. & Chan-Frazier, V.L. (2017). *Greek life on campus: An asset and a challenge.* Retrieved from http://www.insightintodiversity.com/greek-life-on-campus-an-asset-and-a-challenge/

National Research Council. (1995). *The Land Grant Universities: A Profile.* Washington, D.C.: National Academy Press

National Survey of Student Engagement. (2018). *About NSSE.* Retrieved from http://nsse.indiana.edu/html/about.cfm

Nelson, K. (2017). *The importance of student leadership.* Retrieved from https://aboutleaders.com/student-leadership/#gs.HIEOigk

Neumann, A., Terosky, A.L., & Schell, J. (2006). Agents of learning. In S.J. Bracken, J.K. Allen, & D.R. Dean. *The balancing act: Gendered perspectives in faculty roles and work lives,* (pp. 91-120). Sterling, VA: Stylus Publishing

New, J. (2016). Civic learning. *Inside Higher Ed.* Retrieved from https://www.insidehighered.com/news/2016/05/10/colleges-placing-increasing-importance-programs-promoting-civic-engagement

Newman, L. A., & Madaus, J. W. (2015). An analysis of factors related to receipt of accommodations and services by postsecondary students with disabilities. *Remedial and Special Education, 36*(4), 208–219.

Nilson, L.B. (2017). *Getting students to do the readings.* Retrieved from http://www.nea.org/home/34689.htm

Novak, J.D. & Gowin, D.B. (1984). *Learning how to learn.* New York, NY: Cambridge University Press.

Nygaard, C., Brand, S., Batholomew, P., & Millard, L. (2013). *Student engagement: Identity, motivation and community.* Oxfordshire, UK: Libri Publishing

Ohrablo, S. (2018). *High-impact advising: A guide for academic advisors.* Denver, CO: Academic Impressions.

O'Meara, K., Terosky, A.L., & Neumann, A. (2008). *Faculty careers and work lives: A professional growth perspective.* Hoboken, NJ: Wiley Periodicals, Inc.

Pascarella, E.T., & Terenzini, P.T. (2005). *How college affects students: A third decade of research.* San Francisco, CA: Jossey-Bass.

Patton, L.D., Renn, K.A., Guido, F.M., & Quaye, S.J. (2016). *Student development in college: Theory, research, and practice* (3rd ed.). San Francisco, CA: Jossey-Bass

Pearson. (2018). *The best way to increase student engagement in your classroom.* Retrieved from https://www.pearsoned.com/best-way-increase-student-engagement-classroom/

Pescosolido, B.A. (1994). Society and the balance of professional dominance, and patient autonomy in medical care. *Indiana Law Journal, 69*(4), 12. Retrieved from https://www.repository.law.indiana.edu/ilj/vol69/iss4/12/

Philipsen, M.I., & Bostic, T.B. (2010). *Helping faculty find work-life balance: The path toward family-friendly institutions.* San Francisco. CA: Jossey-Bass.

Pines, A. & Aronson, E. (1988). *Career burnout: Causes and cures.* New York, NY: Free Press.

Pinto, C. (2018). *The importance of mentors and meaningful professional development.* Retrieved from http://blogs.edweek.org/teachers/new_teacher_chat/2018/04/the_importance_of_mentors_and_.html

Posner, B.Z. (2018). *Becoming an exemplary student leader.* Retrieved from https://www.collegexpress.com/articles-and-advice/student-life/articles/student-activities/becoming-exemplary-student-leader/

Preston, M.M. (2017). *Teaching context: A map for course design.* Retrieved from http://www.nea.org/home/34714.htm

Project Pericles, Inc. (2018). *Creating cohesive pathways to civic engagement.* Retrieved from http://www.projectpericles.org/projectpericles/programs/Creating_Cohesive_Pathways/

Public Agenda. (2017). *Success is what counts: A community college guide to community engagement and strategic partnerships.* Retrieved from https://www.publicagenda.org/files/PublicAgenda_SuccessIsWhatCounts_Guide_2017.pdf

Putnam, J. & Rathburn, S. (2017). *Advising a clear pathway to high-impact practices with faculty partners.* Retrieved from http://www.nacada.ksu.edu/Resources/Academic-Advising-Today/View-Articles/Advising-a-Clear-Pathway-to-High-Impact-Practices-with-Faculty-Partners.aspx

Quality Assurance Agency. (2012). *Understanding the barriers to student engagement.* Retrieved from http://www.aqa.ac.nz/sites/all/files/Understanding-the-barriers-to-student-engagement-August-2012.pdf

Quaye, S.J. & Harper, S.R. (2015). *Student engagement in higher education: Theoretical perspectives and practical approaches for diverse learners* (2nd ed.). New York, NY: Routledge.

Ravisini, C. (2017). *Why student leadership is important in education?.* Retrieved from http://www.btac.nsw.edu.au/2017/02/student-leadership-important-education/

Ready Education. (2016). *Top 3 tips for an awesome student orientation.* Retrieved from http://blog.oohlalamobile.com/2016/01/top-3-tips-for-an-awesome-student-orientation/

Reich, J.W., Zautra, A.J. & Stuart, J. (2010). *Handbook of adult resilience.* New York, NY: Guilford Press.

Rendon, L.I. (1994). Validating culturally diverse students: Toward a new model of learning and student development. *Innovative Higher Education, 19,* 33-51. DOI: 10.1007/BF01191156

Reynolds, M.M. (2010). *An advisor's half dozen: Principles for incorporating learning theory into our advising practices.* Retrieved from https://www.nacada.ksu.edu/Resources/Clearinghouse/View-Articles/Learning-theory-in-academic-advising.aspx

Rhone, M. (2018). *College student engagement: extracurricular activities help in multiple ways.* Retrieved from http://www.stateuniversity.com/blog/permalink/college-student-engagement-extracurricular-activities-help-in-multiple-ways.html

Richardson, L. (2017). Turning your classroom inside out. *NEA Higher Education Advocate.* Retrieved from http://www.nea.org/assets/docs/HE/Thriving.May12.pdf

Robsham, K. (2016). *Institutional strategies to increase college student engagement.* Retrieved from http://www.presence.io/blog/institutional-strategies-to-increase-college-student-engagement/

Roy, L., Escalera, L., Fernandez, S., Korbek-Erdogmus, E., Reid, J., Bush, A. & Saltmarsh., J. (2017). *Designing a high-impact college for returning adult students.* Retrieved from https://www.aacu.org/diversitydemocracy/2017/fall/roy

Rutter, M.P. & Mintz, S. (2016). The curricular and co-curricular. *Inside Higher Ed.* Retrieved from https://www.insidehighered.com/blogs/higher-ed-gamma/curricular-and-co-curricular

Sakulku, J., & Alexander, J. (2011). The imposter phenomenon. *International Journal of Behavioral Science, 6*(1), 75-97. DOI: 10.14456/ijbs.2011.6

Sanford, N. (1966). *Self and society: Social change and individual development.* New York, NY: Atherton.

Schell, J.A. & Butler, A.C. (2018). *Insights from the science of learning can inform evidence-based implementation of peer instruction.* DOI: 10.3389/feduc.2018.00033/full

Schlechty Center on Engagement. (n.d.). *Working on the work framework.* Retrieved from https://www.rcsdk12.org/cms/lib/NY01001156/Centricity/Domain/1053/sc_pdf_engagement.pdf

Schlechty, P. C. (2002). Working on the work: An action plan for teachers, principals, and superintendents. San Francisco: Jossey-Bass

Schlechty, P.C. (2011). *Engaging students: The next level of working on the work.* San Francisco, CA: Jossey-Bass

Schlossberg, N.K. (1989). *Marginality and Mattering: Key issues in building community.* Retrieved from http://citeseerx.ist.psu.edu/viewdoc/download?doi=10.1.1.842.3826&rep=rep1&type=pdf

Schon, D.A. (1987). *Educating the Reflective Practitioner: Toward a New Design for Teaching and Learning in the Professionals.* San Francisco, CA: Jossey-Bass.

Schreiner, L. (2013). Strengths-based advising. In Drake, J.K., Jordan, P., & Miller, M.A. (Eds.). *Academic Advising Approaches: Strategies that Teach Students to Make the Most of College,* (pp.105-120). San Francisco, CA: Jossey-Bass.

Schubert-Irastorza, C., & Fabry, D.L. (2014). Job satisfaction, burnout, and work engagement in higher education. *Journal of Research in Innovative Teaching, 7*(1), p. 37-50. Retrieved from https://www.nu.edu/assets/resources/pageResources/journal-of-research-in-innovative-teaching-volume-7.pdf

Schwartz, M. (2018). *Increasing faculty-student engagement.* Retrieved from https://www.ryerson.ca/content/dam/lt/resources/handouts/FacultyStudentEngagement.pdf

Scudamore, B. (2016). Why team building is the most important investment you'll make. *Forbes.* Retrieved from https://www.forbes.com/sites/brianscudamore/2016/03/09/why-team-building-is-the-most-important-investment-youll-make/#3c51c9ef617f

Shupp, M.R. (2014). *Rethinking new student orientation.* Retrieved from https://www.wsac.wa.gov/sites/default/files/2014.ptw.(36).pdf

Silverman, A. (2017). *How to create a summer bridge program that actually works.* Retrieved from https://www.eab.com/blogs/enrollment/2017/03/how-to-create-a-summer-bridge-program-that-actually-works

Skovholt, T.M. & Trotter-Mathison M. (2016). *The resilient practitioner: Burnout and compassion, fatigue prevention and self-care strategies for the helping professions* (3rd ed.). New York, NY: Routledge.

Sorcinelli, M.D. (1991). *Research findings on the seven principles.* Retrieved from https://onlinelibrary.wiley.com/doi/abs/10.1002/tl.37219914704

Southern Methodist University. (n.d.). *Using technology to enhance teaching & learning.* Retrieved from https://www.smu.edu/Provost/CTE/Resources/Technology

Sternberg, A. (2018, May 27). The cure for New York face. *New York Magazine,* 22-29. Retrieved from https://www.scribd.com/article/380212594/The-Cure-For-New-York-Face

Strang, T. (2013). *Tips for students: Leadership qualities – Staying on target.* Retrieved from https://blog.cengage.com/top_blog/tips-for-students-leadership-qualities-staying-on-target/

Strayhorn, T.L. (2012). *College students' sense of belonging: A key to educational success for all students.* New York, NY: Routledge.

Sue, D.W. (2001). Multicultural facets of cultural competence. *The Counseling Psychologist, 29*(6), 790-821. DOI: 10.1177/0011000001296002

Sue, D.W., Bernier, J.E., Durran, A., Feinberg, L., Pedersen, P., Smith, E.J., & Vasquez-Nuttall, E. (1982). Position paper: Cross-cultural counseling competencies. *The Counseling Psychologist, 10*(2), 45-52. DOI: 10.1177/0011000082102008

Swail, W.S., Quinn, K., Landis, K., & Fung, M. (2012). A blueprint for success: Case studies of successful pre-college outreach programs. *Educational Policy Institute.* Retrieved from http://www.educationalpolicy.org/publications/pubpdf/TG_CASESTUDY.pdf

Tagg, J. (2012). Why does the faculty resist change? *Change: The Magazine of Higher Learning.* Retrieved from http://web.peralta.edu/pbi/files/2010/11/John-Tagg-article-Jan-2012.pdf

Tenhouse, A.M. (2018). *College extracurricular activities – Impact on students, types of activities.* Retrieved from http://education.stateuniversity.com/pages/1855/College-Extracurricular-Activities.html

Terenzini, P.T., Rendon, L.I., Upcraft, M.L., Millar, J., Allison, K., Gregg, P., & Jalomo, R. (1994). The transition to college: Diverse students, diverse stories. *Research in Higher Education, 37,* 1-22. DOI: 10.1007/BF02496662

The American Institute of Stress. (2018). *Definitions.* Retrieved from https://www.stress.org/military/for-practitionersleaders/compassion-fatigue/

The Center for Generational Kinetics. (2017). *The state of gen z 2017: Meet the throwback generation.* Retrieved from https://genhq.com/gen-z/

The Mindset List. (2018). *Class of 2019.* Retrieved from http://themindsetlist.com/2015/08/the-beloit-college-mindset-list-class-of-2019-born-1997/

The Quad. (2018). *Joining a fraternity or sorority: The pros and cons of Greek life*. Retrieved from https://thebestschools.org/magazine/joining-a-fraternity-or-sorority-real-pros-and-cons-of-greek-life/

Tinto, V. (1993). *Leaving college: Rethinking the causes and cures of student attrition*. Chicago, IL: University of Chicago Press.

Tinto, V. (2000). Linking learning and leaving: Exploring the role of the college classroom in student departure. In J.M. Braxton (Ed.), *Reworking the student departure puzzle*, (pp. 81-94). Nashville, TN: Vanderbilt University Press.

Tinto, V. (2005). Reflecting on student retention and persistence. *Studies in Learning, Evaluation, Innovation, and Development, 2*(3). Retrieved from http://shiftwork.cqu.edu.au/viewarticle.php?id=103

Tinto, V. (2012). Enhancing student success: Taking the classroom success seriously. *The International Journal of the First Year in Higher Education, 3*(1), 1-8. DOI: 10.5204/intjfhye.v2i1119

Tomasiewicz, R. (2017). Advising special populations in the first year. In J.R. Fox & H.E. Martin (Eds.). *Academic Advising and the First College Year*, (pp.127-149). Sterling, VA: Stylus Publishing

Trevino, M. (2018). *Establishing habits of engagement from orientation to commencement-moving from involvement to engagement* [video file]. Retrieved from http://www.campusintelligence.com/recorded_webinars/establishing-habits-of-engagement-from-orientation-to-commencement/

Turley, N. (October 7, 2013). *Mental health issues among graduate students*. Retrieved from https://www.insidehighered.com/blogs/gradhacker/mental-health-issues-among-graduate-students

U.S. Department of Education. (2017). *Reimagining the role of technology in education: 2017 national education technology plan update*. Retrieved from https://tech.ed.gov/files/2017/01/NETP17.pdf

U.S. Department of Education. (2016). *Summer bridge programs*. Retrieved from https://ies.ed.gov/ncee/wwc/Docs/InterventionReports/wwc_summerbridge_071916.pdf

Umbach, P.D., & Wawrzynski, M.R. (2004). *Faculty do matter: The role of college faculty in student learning and engagement*. Retrieved from nsse.indiana.edu/pdf/research_papers/faculty_do_matter.pdf

University of Minnesota. (2018). *Benefits of service-learning*. Center for community-engaged learning. Retrieved from http://www.servicelearning.umn.edu/info/benefits.html

University of Wisconsin-Stevens Point. (2018). *What is Greek Life?* Retrieved from https://www.uwsp.edu/centers/CASE/pages/greek/what-is-greek.aspx

van Saane, N., Sluiter J.K., Verbeek, J.H.A.M., & Frings-Dresen, M.H.W. (2003). Reliability and validity of instruments measuring job satisfaction- a systematic review. *Occupational Machine, 53*, 191-200. DOI: 10.1093/occmed/kqg038.

Varney, J. (2007). Intrusive advising. *NACADA: Academic Advising Today, 30*(3). Retrieved from https://www.nacada.ksu.edu/Resources/Academic-Advising-Today/View-Articles/Intrusive-Advising.aspx

Varney, J. (2013). Proactive advising. In Drake, J.K., Jordan, P., & Miller, M.A. (Eds.). *Academic Advising Approaches: Strategies that Teach Students to Make the Most of College*, (pp.137-145). San Francisco, CA: Jossey-Bass.

Villegas-Reimers, E. (nd.). *Creating Learning Communities that engage students in the college and its surrounding communities in meaningful community service as a strategy to develop students' persistence in college.* Retrieved from www2.ed.gov/documents/college-completion/wheelock-college.doc

Walton, G.M. & Cohen, G.L. (2011). A brief social-belonging intervention improves academic and health outcomes of minority students. *Science, 331*(6023), 1447-1451. DOI: 10.1126/science.1198364

Wang, M.C. & Gordon, E.W. (1994). *Educational Resilience in inner-city America: Challenges and prospects.* Mahwah, NJ: Lawrence Erlbaum Associates.

Watts, J. & Robertson, N. (2011). Burnout in university teaching staff: A systematic literature review. *Educational Research, 53*(1), 33-50. DOI: 10.1080/00131881.2011.552235

Webber, K.L., Krylow, R.B., & Zhang, Q. (2013). Does involvement really matter? Indicators of college student success and satisfaction. *Journal of Student Development, 54*(6), 591-611. Retrieved from http://ihe.uga.edu/uploads/publications/faculty/Does_Involvement_Really_Matter.pdf

Weimer, M. (2012). *10 ways to promote student engagement.* Retrieved from https://www.facultyfocus.com/articles/effective-teaching-strategies/10-ways-to-promote-student-engagement/

Werner, E.E. & Smith, R.S. (1982). *Vulnerable but invincible: A study of resilient children.* New York, NY: McGraw-Hill.

Wertalik, D. (2017). Social media and building a connected college. *Cogent Business & Management,* 4:1. DOI: 10.1080/23311975.2017.1320836

Whitebook, M. & Bellum, D. (2014). Mentors as teachers, learners, and leaders. *Exchange Press,* 14-18. Retrieved from http://cscce.berkeley.edu/files/2014/FINAL-218-Whitebook-Bellm1.pdf

Wicks, J.R. (2018). *Using collaboration theory to address the "how" of relational core competencies.* Retrieved from https://www.nacada.ksu.edu/Resources/Academic-Advising-Today/View-Articles/Using-Collaboration-Theory-to-Address-the-How-of-Relational-Core-Competencies.aspx

Wiley, J. (2018). *Symbiotic benefits: How improving strategic student engagement impacts institutions and students alike.* Retrieved from https://evolllution.com/attracting-students/retention/symbiotic-benefits-how-improving-strategic-student-engagement-impacts-institutions-and-students-alike/

Winston, R. B., Jr., Miller, T. K., Ender, S. C., & Grites, T. J. (Eds.). (1982). *Developmental academic advising.* San Francisco, CA: Jossey-Bass.

Wither, D. (2016). *Why the best leaders delegate?* Retrieved from https://www.entrepreneur.com/article/279141

Wolin, S., & Wolin, S. (2010). *The resilient self.* Random House Publishers.

Wondergem, K. (2017). *Here comes Z: Strategies to engage a new generation of college students.* Retrieved from https://elearningindustry.com/engage-a-new-generation-of-college-students-strategies

Wong, A. (2015). The activity gap. *The Atlantic.* Retrieved from https://www.theatlantic.com/education/archive/2015/01/the-activity-gap/384961/

Xu, D., Ran, F.X., Fink, J., Jenkins, D., & Dundar, A. (2018). Collaboratively clearing the path to a baccalaureate degree: Identifying effective 2- to 4-year college transfer partnerships. *Sage Journals, 46*(3), 231-256. DOI: 10.1177/0091552118772649

Young, N.D., Celli, L.M., & Mumby, M.A. (2019). *Educating the experienced: Challenges and best practices in adult learning.* Madison, WI: Atwood Publishing

Young, N.D., Jean (Bienia), E. & Quayson, F. (2017). *From Lecture Hall to Laptop: Opportunities, Challenges, and the continuing Evolution of Virtual Learning in Higher Education.* Madison, IL: Atwood.

Young, N.D., & Michael, C.N. (2009*). Counseling with confidence: From pre-service to professional practice. Amherst, MA:* The Psychosynthesis Press.

Young, N.D., Michael, C.N., & Jean, E. (2018). *Dog Tags to Diploma: Understanding and Addressing the Educational Needs of Veterans, Service Member and their Families.* Madison, WI: Atwood.

Youssef, C.M. & Luthans, F. (2007). Positive Organizational Behavior in the Workplace: The Impact of Hope, Optimism, and Resilience. *Management Department Faculty Publications.* Paper 36. http://digitalcommons.unl.edu/managementfacpub/36

Zenger, J. (2015). Taking responsibility is the highest mark of great leaders. *Forbes.* Retrieved from https://www.forbes.com/sites/jackzenger/2015/07/16/taking-responsibility-is-the-highest-mark-of-great-leaders/#309d415948f2

Zepke, N., & Leach, L. (2010). Improving student engagement: Ten proposals for action. *Active Learning in Higher Education, 11*(3), 167-177. DOI: 10.1177/1469787410379680

Zhang, N. (2016). *Rentz's student affairs practice in higher* education (5th ed.). Springfield, IL: Charles C. Thomas Publishers

Zobel, E.J. (2016). *The correlation between college student engagement and 1st to 2nd year retention.* Retrieved from https://d-commons.d.umn.edu/bitstream/10792/3236/1/Zobel%2C%20Emily.pdf

Zohar, I. (2015). The art of negotiation leadership skills required for negotiation in time of crisis. *Procedia: Social and Behavioral Sciences,* 209(3), 540-548. DOI: 10.1016/j.sbspro.2015.11.285

About the Authors

Nicholas D. Young, PhD, EdD

Dr. Nicholas D. Young has worked in diverse educational roles for more than 30 years, serving as a principal, special education director, graduate professor, graduate program director, graduate dean, and longtime superintendent of schools. He was named the Massachusetts Superintendent of the Year; and he completed a distinguished Fulbright program focused on the Japanese educational system through the collegiate level. Dr. Young is the recipient of numerous other honors and recognitions including the General Douglas MacArthur Award for distinguished civilian and military leadership and the Vice Admiral John T. Hayward Award for exemplary scholarship. He holds several graduate degrees including a PhD in educational administration and an EdD in educational psychology.

Dr. Young has served in the U.S. Army and U.S. Army Reserves combined for over 34 years; and he graduated with distinction from the U.S. Air War College, the U.S. Army War College, and the U.S. Navy War College. After completing a series of senior leadership assignments in the U.S. Army Reserves as the commanding officer of the 287th Medical Company (DS), the 405th Area Support Company (DS), the 405th Combat Support Hospital, and the 399th Combat Support Hospital, he transitioned to his current military position as a faculty instructor at the U.S. Army War College in Carlisle, PA. He currently holds the rank of Colonel.

Dr. Young is also a regular presenter at state, national, and international conferences; and he has written many books, book chapters, and/or articles on various topics in education, counseling, and psychology. Some of his most recent books include *Educating the Experienced: Challenges and Best Practices in Adult Learning* (2019); *Securing the Schoolyard: Protocols that Promote Safety and Positive Student Behaviors* (2019); *Sounding the Alarm in the Schoolhouse: Safety, Security and Student Well-Being* (2019); *The Soul of the Schoolhouse: Cultivating Student Engagement* (2019); *Embracing and Educating the Autistic Child: Valuing Those Who Color Outside the Lines* (2019); *From Cradle to Classroom: A Guide to Special Education for Young Children* (2019); *Captivating Classrooms: Educational

Strategies to Enhance Student Engagement (2019); *Potency of the Principalship: Action-Oriented Leadership at the Heart of School Improvement* (2018); *Soothing the Soul: Pursuing a Life of Abundance Through a Practice of Gratitude* (2018); *Dog Tags to Diploma: Understanding and Addressing the Educational Needs of Veterans, Servicemembers, and their Families* (2018); *Turbulent Times: Confronting Challenges in Emerging Adulthood* (2018); *Guardians of the Next Generation: Igniting the Passion for Quality Teaching* (2018); *Achieving Results: Maximizing Success in the Schoolhouse* (2018); *From Head to Heart: High Quality Teaching Practices in the Spotlight* (2018); *Stars in the Schoolhouse: Teaching Practices and Approaches that Make a Difference* (2018); *Making the Grade: Promoting Positive Outcomes for Students with Learning Disabilities* (2018); *Paving the Pathway for Educational Success: Effective Classroom Interventions for Students with Learning Disabilities* (2018); *Wrestling with Writing: Effective Strategies for Struggling Students* (2018); *Floundering to Fluent: Reaching and Teaching the Struggling Student* (2018); *Emotions and Education: Promoting Positive Mental Health in Students with Learning* (2018); *From Lecture Hall to Laptop: Opportunities, Challenges, and the Continuing Evolution of Virtual Learning in Higher Education* (2017); *The Power of the Professoriate: Demands, Challenges, and Opportunities in 21st Century Higher Education* (2017); *To Campus with Confidence: Supporting a Successful Transition to College for Students with Learning Disabilities* (2017); *Educational Entrepreneurship: Promoting Public-Private Partnerships for the 21st Century* (2015); *Beyond the Bedtime Story: Promoting Reading Development during the Middle School Years* (2015); *Betwixt and Between: Understanding and Meeting the Social and Emotional Developmental Needs of Students During the Middle School Transition Years* (2014); *Learning Style Perspectives: Impact Upon the Classroom* (3rd ed., 2014); and *Collapsing Educational Boundaries from Preschool to PhD: Building Bridges Across the Educational Spectrum* (2013); *Transforming Special Education Practices: A Primer for School Administrators and Policy Makers* (2012); and *Powerful Partners in Student Success: Schools, Families and Communities* (2012). He also co-authored several children's books to include the popular series *I am Full of Possibilities*. Dr. Young may be contacted directly at nyoung1191@aol.com.

Christine N. Michael, PhD

Dr. Christine N. Michael is a more than 40-year educational veteran with a variety of professional experiences. She holds degrees from Brown University, Rhode Island College, Union Institute and University, and the

University of Connecticut, where she earned a PhD in education, human development, and family relations. Her previous work has included middle and high school teaching, higher education administration, college teaching, and educational consulting. She has also been involved with Head Start, Upward Bound, national non-profits Foundation for Excellent Schools and College for Every Student, and the federal Trio programs. She is currently the Program Director of Low Residency Programs at American International College.

Dr. Michael has published widely on topics in education and psychology. Her most recent works included serving as a primary author on the book *Securing the Schoolyard: Protocols that Promote Safety and Positive Student Behaviors* (2019); *Sounding the Alarm in the Schoolhouse: Safety, Security and Student Well-Being* (2019); *The Soul of the Schoolhouse: Cultivating Student Engagement* (2019); *Captivating Classrooms: Educational Strategies to Enhance Student Engagement* (2019); *Turbulent Times: Confronting Challenges in Emerging Adulthood* (2018); *To Campus with Confidence: Supporting a Successful Transition to College for Students with Learning Disabilities* (2017), *Beyond the Bedtime Story: Promoting Reading Development during the Middle School Years* (2015), *Betwixt and Between: Understanding and Meeting the Social and Emotional Development Needs of Students During the Middle School Transition Years* (2014), and *Powerful Partners in Student Success: Schools, Families and Communities* (2012). Dr. Michael may be contacted at cnevadam@gmail.com.

Jennifer A. Smolinski, J.D.

Attorney Jennifer Smolinski has worked in education for more than three years. Her role within higher education includes the creation of, and coordinator for, the Center for Accessibility Services and Academic Accommodations at American International College located in Springfield, Massachusetts. She has also taught criminal justice and legal research and writing classes within the field of higher education. Prior to her work at the collegiate level, Attorney Smolinski worked as a solo-practitioner conducting education and disability advocacy.

Attorney Smolinski received a Bachelor of Arts in Anthropology and Bachelor of Arts in Sociology from the University of Connecticut, a Master in Psychology and Counseling as well as a Master of Higher Education Student Affairs from Salem State University and her law degree from Massachusetts School of Law. She is currently an EdD in Educational Leadership and Supervision candidate at American International College, where she is focusing her research on special education and laws to protect students with disabilities in the classroom.

Attorney Smolinski has become a regular presenter educating the faculty, staff and students at institutes of higher education on disabilities and accommodations at the collegiate level and has presented to local high school special education departments on the transition to college under the Americans with Disabilities Act. She has co-authored *Securing the Schoolyard: Protocols that Promote Safety and Positive Student Behaviors* (2019); *Sounding the Alarm in the Schoolhouse: Safety, Security and Student Well-Being* (2019); *Captivating Classrooms: Educational Strategies to Enhance Student Engagement* (2019); *Guardian of the Next Generation: Igniting the Passion for Quality Teaching* (2018); and *Making the Grade: Promoting Positive Outcomes for Students with Learning Disabilities* (2018). She can be reached at Jennifer.Smolinski@aic.edu.

www.ingramcontent.com/pod-product-compliance
Lightning Source LLC
Chambersburg PA
CBHW061448300426
44114CB00014B/1893